Three Plays

THREE PLAYS

BY

Harold Pinter

A SLIGHT ACHE
THE COLLECTION
THE DWARFS

GROVE PRESS, INC.
NEW YORK

TO VIVIEN

Three Plays

A Slight Ache

A Slight Ache was first performed on the B.B.C. Third Programme on 29 July 1959, with the following cast:

EDWARD   Maurice Denham
FLORA   Vivien Merchant

Produced by Donald McWhinnie

It was presented by Michael Codron at the Arts Theatre, London, on 18 January 1961, and subsequently at the Criterion Theatre, with the following cast:

EDWARD   Emlyn Williams
FLORA   Alison Leggat
MATCHSELLER   Richard Briers

Produced by Donald McWhinnie

A Slight Ache

A country house, with two chairs and a table laid for breakfast at the centre of the stage. These will later be removed and the action will be focused on the scullery on the right and the study on the left, both indicated with a minimum of scenery and props. A large well kept garden is suggested at the back of the stage with flower beds, trimmed hedges, etc. The garden gate, which cannot be seen by the audience, is off right.

FLORA *and* EDWARD *are discovered sitting at the breakfast table.* EDWARD *is reading the paper.*

FLORA: Have you noticed the honeysuckle this morning?

EDWARD: The what?

FLORA: The honeysuckle.

EDWARD: Honeysuckle? Where?

FLORA: By the back gate, Edward.

EDWARD: Is that honeysuckle? I thought it was . . . convolvulus, or something.

FLORA: But you know it's honeysuckle.

EDWARD: I tell you I thought it was convolvulus.

[*Pause.*]

FLORA: It's in wonderful flower.

EDWARD: I must look.

FLORA: The whole garden's in flower this morning. The clematis. The convolvulus. Everything. I was out at seven. I stood by the pool.

EDWARD: Did you say—that the convolvulus was in flower?

FLORA: Yes.

EDWARD: But good God, you just denied there was any.

FLORA: I was talking about the honeysuckle.

EDWARD: About the what?

FLORA [calmly]: Edward—you know that shrub outside the toolshed . . .

EDWARD: Yes, yes.

FLORA: That's convolvulus.

EDWARD: That?

FLORA: Yes.

EDWARD: Oh.

[Pause.]

I thought it was japonica.

FLORA: Oh, good Lord no.

EDWARD: Pass the teapot, please.

Pause. She pours tea for him.

I don't see why I should be expected to distinguish between these plants. It's not my job.

FLORA: You know perfectly well what grows in your garden.

EDWARD: Quite the contrary. It is clear that I don't.

[Pause.]

FLORA [rising]: I was up at seven. I stood by the pool. The peace. And everything in flower. The sun was up. You should work in the garden this morning. We could put up the canopy.

EDWARD: The canopy? What for?

FLORA: To shade you from the sun.

EDWARD: Is there a breeze?

FLORA: A light one.

EDWARD: It's very treacherous weather, you know.

[Pause.]

FLORA: Do you know what today is?

EDWARD: Saturday.

FLORA: It's the longest day of the year.

EDWARD: Really?

FLORA: It's the height of summer today.

EDWARD: Cover the marmalade.

FLORA: What?

EDWARD: Cover the pot. There's a wasp. [*He puts the paper down on the table.*] Don't move. Keep still. What are you doing?

FLORA: Covering the pot.

EDWARD: Don't move. Leave it. Keep still.

[*Pause.*]

Give me the 'Telegraph'.

FLORA: Don't hit it. It'll bite.

EDWARD: Bite? What do you mean, bite? Keep still.

[*Pause.*]

It's landing.

FLORA: It's going in the pot.

EDWARD: Give me the lid.

FLORA: It's in.

EDWARD: Give me the lid.

FLORA: I'll do it.

EDWARD: Give it to me! Now . . . Slowly . . .

FLORA: What are you doing?

EDWARD: Be quiet. Slowly . . . carefully . . . on . . . the . . . pot! Ha-ha-ha. Very good.

He sits on a chair to the right of the table.

FLORA: Now he's in the marmalade.

EDWARD: Precisely.

Pause. She sits on a chair to the left of the table and reads the 'Telegraph'.

FLORA: Can you hear him?

EDWARD: Hear him?

FLORA: Buzzing.

EDWARD: Nonsense. How can you hear him? It's an earthenware lid.

FLORA: He's becoming frantic.

EDWARD: Rubbish. Take it away from the table.

FLORA: What shall I do with it?

EDWARD: Put it in the sink and drown it.

FLORA: It'll fly out and bite me.

EDWARD: It will not bite you! Wasps don't bite. Anyway, it won't fly out. It's stuck. It'll drown where it is, in the marmalade.

FLORA: What a horrible death.

EDWARD: On the contrary.

[*Pause.*]

FLORA: Have you got something in your eyes?

EDWARD: No. Why do you ask?

FLORA: You keep clenching them, blinking them.

EDWARD: I have a slight ache in them.

FLORA: Oh, dear.

EDWARD: Yes, a slight ache. As if I hadn't slept.

FLORA: Did you sleep, Edward?

EDWARD: Of course I slept. Uninterrupted. As always.

FLORA: And yet you feel tired.

EDWARD: I didn't say I felt tired. I merely said I had a slight ache in my eyes.

FLORA: Why is that, then?

EDWARD: I really don't know.

[*Pause.*]

FLORA: Oh goodness!

EDWARD: What is it?

FLORA: I can see it. It's trying to come out.

EDWARD: How can it?

FLORA: Through the hole. It's trying to crawl out, through the spoon-hole.

EDWARD: Mmmnn, yes. Can't do it, of course. [*Silent pause.*] Well, let's kill it, for goodness' sake.

FLORA: Yes, let's. But how?

EDWARD: Bring it out on the spoon and squash it on a plate.

FLORA: It'll fly away. It'll bite.

EDWARD: If you don't stop saying that word I shall leave this table.

FLORA: But wasps do bite.

EDWARD: They don't bite. They sting. It's snakes . . . that bite.

FLORA: What about horseflies?

[*Pause.*]

EDWARD [*to himself*]: Horseflies suck.

[*Pause.*]

FLORA [*tentatively*]: If we . . . if we wait long enough, I suppose it'll choke to death. It'll suffocate in the marmalade.

EDWARD [*briskly*]: You do know I've got work to do this morning, don't you? I can't spend the whole day worrying about a wasp.

FLORA: Well, kill it.

EDWARD: You want to kill it?

FLORA: Yes.

EDWARD: Very well. Pass me the hot water jug.

FLORA: What are you going to do?

EDWARD: Scald it. Give it to me.

She hands him the jug. Pause.

Now . . .

FLORA [*whispering*]: Do you want me to lift the lid?

EDWARD: No, no, no. I'll pour down the spoon hole. Right . . . down the spoon-hole.

FLORA: Listen!

EDWARD: What?

FLORA: It's buzzing.

EDWARD: Vicious creatures.

[*Pause.*]

Curious, but I don't remember seeing any wasps at all, all

summer, until now. I'm sure I don't know why. I mean, there must have been wasps.

FLORA: Please.

EDWARD: This couldn't be the first wasp, could it?

FLORA: Please.

EDWARD: The first wasp of summer? No. It's not possible.

FLORA: Edward.

EDWARD: Mmmmnnn?

FLORA: Kill it.

EDWARD: Ah, yes. Tilt the pot. Tilt. Aah . . . down here . . . right down . . . blinding him . . . that's . . . it.

FLORA: Is it?

EDWARD: Lift the lid. All right, I will. There he is! Dead. What a monster. [*He squashes it on a plate.*]

FLORA: What an awful experience.

EDWARD: What a beautiful day it is. Beautiful. I think I shall work in the garden this morning. Where's that canopy?

FLORA: It's in the shed.

EDWARD: Yes, we must get it out. My goodness, just look at that sky. Not a cloud. Did you say it was the longest day of the year today?

FLORA: Yes.

EDWARD: Ah, it's a good day. I feel it in my bones. In my muscles. I think I'll stretch my legs in a minute. Down to the pool. My God, look at that flowering shrub over there. Clematis. What a wonderful . . . [*He stops suddenly.*]

FLORA: What?

[*Pause.*]

Edward, what is it?

[*Pause.*]

Edward . . .

EDWARD [*thickly*]: He's there.

FLORA: Who?

EDWARD [*low, murmuring*]: Blast and damn it, he's there, he's there at the back gate.

FLORA: Let me see.

She moves over to him to look. Pause.

[*Lightly.*] Oh, it's the matchseller.

EDWARD: He's back again.

FLORA: But he's always there.

EDWARD: Why? What is he doing there?

FLORA: But he's never disturbed you, has he? The man's been standing there for weeks. You've never mentioned it.

EDWARD: What is he doing there?

FLORA: He's selling matches, of course.

EDWARD: It's ridiculous. What's the time?

FLORA: Half past nine.

EDWARD: What in God's name is he doing with a tray full of matches at half past nine in the morning?

FLORA: He arrives at seven o'clock.

EDWARD: Seven o'clock?

FLORA: He's always there at seven.

EDWARD: Yes, but you've never . . . actually seen him arrive?

FLORA: No, I . . .

EDWARD: Well, how do you know he's . . . not been standing there all night?

[*Pause.*]

FLORA: Do you find him interesting, Edward?

EDWARD [*casually*]: Interesting? No. No, I . . . don't find him interesting.

FLORA: He's a very nice old man, really.

EDWARD: You've spoken to him?

FLORA: No. No, I haven't spoken to him. I've nodded.

EDWARD [*pacing up and down*]: For two months he's been standing on that spot, do you realize that? Two months. I haven't been able to step outside the back gate.

FLORA: Why on earth not?

EDWARD [*to himself*]: It used to give me great pleasure, such pleasure, to stroll along through the long grass, out through

the back gate, pass into the lane. That pleasure is now
denied me. It's my own house, isn't it? It's my own gate.

FLORA: I really can't understand this, Edward.

EDWARD: Damn. And do you know I've never seen him sell
one box? Not a box. It's hardly surprising. He's on the
wrong road. It's not a road at all. What is it? It's a lane,
leading to the monastery. Off everybody's route. Even the
monks take a short cut to the village, when they want to
go . . . to the village. No one goes up it. Why doesn't he
stand on the main road if he wants to sell matches, by the
front gate? The whole thing's preposterous.

FLORA [*going over to him*]: I don't know why you're getting so
excited about it. He's a quiet, harmless old man, going
about his business. He's quite harmless.

EDWARD: I didn't say he wasn't harmless. Of course he's
harmless. How could he be other than harmless?

Fade out and silence.

FLORA'S *voice, far in the house, drawing nearer.*

FLORA [*off*]: Edward, where are you? Edward? Where are
you, Edward?

She appears.

Edward?
Edward, what are you doing in the scullery?

EDWARD [*looking through the scullery window*]: Doing?

FLORA: I've been looking everywhere for you. I put up the
canopy ages ago. I came back and you were nowhere to be
seen. Have you been out?

EDWARD: No.

FLORA: Where have you been?

EDWARD: Here.

FLORA: I looked in your study. I even went into the attic.

EDWARD [*tonelessly*]: What would I be doing in the attic?

FLORA: I couldn't imagine what had happened to you. Do
you know it's twelve o'clock?

EDWARD: Is it?

FLORA: I even went to the bottom of the garden, to see if you
were in the toolshed.

EDWARD [*tonelessly*]: What would I be doing in the toolshed?

FLORA: You must have seen me in the garden. You can see
through this window.

EDWARD: Only part of the garden.

FLORA: Yes.

EDWARD: Only a corner of the garden. A very small corner.

FLORA: What are you doing in here?

EDWARD: Nothing. I was digging out some notes, that's all.

FLORA: Notes?

EDWARD: For my essay.

FLORA: Which essay?

EDWARD: My essay on space and time.

FLORA: But . . . I've never . . . I don't know that one.

EDWARD: You don't know it?

FLORA: I thought you were writing one about the Belgian
Congo.

EDWARD: I've been engaged on the dimensionality and con-
tinuity of space . . . and time . . . for years.

FLORA: And the Belgian Congo?

EDWARD [*shortly*]: Never mind about the Belgian Congo.
[*Pause.*]

FLORA: But you don't keep notes in the scullery.

EDWARD: You'd be surprised. You'd be highly surprised.

FLORA: Good Lord, what's that? Is that a bullock let loose?
No. It's the matchseller! My goodness, you can see him
. . . through the hedge. He looks bigger. Have you been
watching him? He looks . . . like a bullock.
[*Pause.*]
Edward?
[*Pause.*]

[*Moving over to him.*] Are you coming outside? I've put up the canopy. You'll miss the best of the day. You can have an hour before lunch.

EDWARD: I've no work to do this morning.

FLORA: What about your essay? You don't intend to stay in the scullery all day, do you?

EDWARD: Get out. Leave me alone.

[*A slight pause.*]

FLORA: Really Edward. You've never spoken to me like that in all your life.

EDWARD: Yes, I have.

FLORA: Oh, Weddie. Beddie-Weddie . . .

EDWARD: Do not call me that!

FLORA: Your eyes are bloodshot.

EDWARD: Damn it.

FLORA: It's too dark in here to peer . . .

EDWARD: Damn.

FLORA: It's so bright outside.

EDWARD: Damn.

FLORA: And it's dark in here.

[*Pause.*]

EDWARD: Christ blast it!

FLORA: You're frightened of him.

EDWARD: I'm not.

FLORA: You're frightened of a poor old man. Why?

EDWARD: I am not!

FLORA: He's a poor, harmless old man.

EDWARD: Aaah my eyes.

FLORA: Let me bathe them.

EDWARD: Keep away.

[*Pause.*]

[*Slowly.*] I want to speak to that man. I want to have a word with him.

[*Pause.*]

It's quite absurd, of course. I really can't tolerate something so . . . absurd, right on my doorstep. I shall not tolerate it. He's sold nothing all morning. No one passed. Yes. A monk passed. A non-smoker. In a loose garment. It's quite obvious he was a non-smoker but still, the man made no effort. He made no effort to clinch a sale, to rid himself of one of his cursed boxes. His one chance, all morning, and he made no effort.

[*Pause.*]

I haven't wasted my time. I've hit, in fact, upon the truth. He's not a matchseller at all. The bastard isn't a matchseller at all. Curious I never realized that before. He's an impostor. I watched him very closely. He made no move towards the monk. As for the monk, the monk made no move towards him. The monk was moving along the lane. He didn't pause, or halt, or in any way alter his step. As for the matchseller—how ridiculous to go on calling him by that title. What a farce. No, there is something very false about that man. I intend to get to the bottom of it. I'll soon get rid of him He can go and ply his trade somewhere else. Instead of standing like a bullock . . . a bullock, outside my back gate.

FLORA: But if he isn't a matchseller, what is his trade?

EDWARD: We'll soon find out.

FLORA: You're going out to speak to him?

EDWARD: Certainly not! Go out to *him*? Certainly . . . not. I'll invite him in here. Into my study. Then we'll . . . get to the bottom of it.

FLORA: Why don't you call the police and have him removed?

He laughs. Pause.

Why don't you call the police, Edward? You could say he was a public nuisance. Although I . . . I can't say I find him a nuisance.

EDWARD: Call him in.

FLORA: Me?

EDWARD: Go out and call him in.

FLORA: Are you serious?

[*Pause.*]

Edward, I could call the police. Or even the vicar.

EDWARD: Go and get him.

She goes out. Silence.

EDWARD *waits.*

FLORA [*in the garden*]: Good morning.

[*Pause.*]

We haven't met. I live in this house here. My husband and I.

[*Pause.*]

I wonder if you could . . . would you care for a cup of tea?

[*Pause.*]

Or a glass of lemon? It must be so dry, standing here.

[*Pause.*]

Would you like to come inside for a little while? It's much cooler. There's something we'd very much like to . . . tell you, that will benefit you. Could you spare a few moments? We won't keep you long.

[*Pause.*]

Might I buy your tray of matches, do you think? We've run out, completely, and we always keep a very large stock. It happens that way, doesn't it? Well, we can discuss it inside. Do come. This way. Ah now, do come. Our house is full of curios, you know. My husband's been rather a collector. We have goose for lunch. Do you care for goose?

She moves to the gate.

Come and have lunch with us. This way. That's . . . right. May I take your arm? There's a good deal of *nettle* inside the gate. [*The* MATCHSELLER *appears.*] Here. This way. Mind now. Isn't it beautiful weather? It's the longest day of the year today.

[*Pause.*]

That's honeysuckle. And that's convolvulus. There's clematis. And do you see that plant by the conservatory? That's japonica.

Silence. She enters the study.

FLORA: He's here.

EDWARD: I know.

FLORA: He's in the hall.

EDWARD: I know he's here. I can smell him.

FLORA: Smell him?

EDWARD: I smelt him when he came under my window. Can't you smell the house now?

FLORA: What are you going to do with him, Edward? You won't be rough with him in any way? He's very old. I'm not sure if he can hear, or even see. And he's wearing the oldest—

EDWARD: I don't want to know what he's wearing.

FLORA: But you'll see for yourself in a minute, if you speak to him.

EDWARD: I shall.

[*Slight pause.*]

FLORA: He's an old man. You won't ... be rough with him?

EDWARD: If he's so old, why doesn't he seek shelter ... from the storm?

FLORA: But there's no storm. It's summer, the longest day ...

EDWARD: There was a storm, last week. A summer storm. He stood without moving, while it raged about him.

FLORA: When was this?

EDWARD: He remained quite still, while it thundered all about him.

[*Pause.*]

FLORA: Edward ... are you sure it's wise to bother about all this?

EDWARD: Tell him to come in.

FLORA: I . . .
EDWARD: Now.

She goes and collects the MATCHSELLER.

FLORA: Hullo. Would you like to go in? I won't be long.
Up these stairs here.
[*Pause.*]
You can have some sherry before lunch.
[*Pause.*]
Shall I take your tray? No. Very well, take it with you.
Just . . . up those stairs. The door at the . . .
[*She watches him move.*]
the door . . .
[*Pause.*]
the door at the top. I'll join you . . . later. [*She goes out.*]

The MATCHSELLER *stands on the threshold of the study.*

EDWARD [*cheerfully*]: Here I am. Where are you?
[*Pause.*]
Don't stand out there, old chap. Come into my study.
[*He rises.*] Come in.

The MATCHSELLER *enters.*

That's right. Mind how you go. That's . . . it. Now.
make yourself comfortable. Thought you might like some
refreshment, on a day like this. Sit down, old man. What
will you have? Sherry? Or what about a double scotch? Eh?
[*Pause.*]
I entertain the villagers annually, as a matter of fact. I'm
not the squire, but they look upon me with some regard.
Don't believe we've got a squire here any more, actually.
Don't know what became of him. Nice old man he was.
Great chess-player, as I remember. Three daughters. The
pride of the county. Flaming red hair. Alice was the eldest.
Sit yourself down, old chap. Eunice I think was number

two. The youngest one was the best of the bunch. Sally.
No, no, wait a minute, no, it wasn't Sally, it was . . .
Fanny. Fanny. A flower. You must be a stranger here.
Unless you lived here once, went on a long voyage and
have lately returned. Do you know the district?
[*Pause.*]
Now, now, you mustn't . . . stand about like that. Take
a seat. Which one would you prefer? We have a great
variety, as you see. Can't stand uniformity. Like different
seats, different backs. Often when I'm working, you know,
I draw up one chair, scribble a few lines, put it by, draw
up another, sit back, ponder, put it by . . . [*absently*]
. . . sit back . . . put it by . . .
[*Pause.*]
I write theological and philosophical essays . . .
[*Pause.*]
Now and again I jot down a few observations on certain
tropical phenomena—not from the same standpoint, of
course. [*Silent pause.*] Yes. Africa, now. Africa's always
been my happy hunting ground. Fascinating country. Do
you know it? I get the impression that you've . . . been
around a bit. Do you by any chance know the Membunza
Mountains? Great range south of Katambaloo. French
Equatorial Africa, if my memory serves me right. Most
extraordinary diversity of flora and fauna. Especially fauna.
I understand in the Gobi Desert you can come across
some very strange sights. Never been there myself. Studied
the maps though. Fascinating things, maps.
[*Pause.*]
Do you live in the village? I don't often go down, of course.
Or are you passing through? On your way to another part
of the country? Well, I can tell you, in my opinion you
won't find many prettier parts than here. We win the first
prize regularly, you know, the best kept village in the area.
Sit down.

[*Pause.*]

I say, can you hear me?

[*Pause.*]

I said, I say, can you hear me?

[*Pause.*]

You possess most extraordinary repose, for a man of your age, don't you? Well, perhaps that's not quite the right word . . . repose. Do you find it chilly in here? I'm sure it's chillier in here than out. I haven't been out yet, today, though I shall probably spend the whole afternoon working, in the garden, under my canopy, at my table, by the pool. [*Pause.*]

Oh, I understand you met my *wife*? Charming woman, don't you think? Plenty of grit there, too. Stood by me through thick and thin, that woman. In season and out of season. Fine figure of a woman she was, too, in her youth. Wonderful carriage, flaming red hair. [*He stops abruptly.*] [*Pause.*]

Yes, I . . . I was in much the same position myself then as you are now, you understand. Struggling to make my way in the world. I was in commerce too. [*With a chuckle.*] Oh, yes, I know what it's like—the weather, the rain, beaten from pillar to post, up hill and down dale . . . the rewards were few . . . winters in hovels . . . up till all hours working at your thesis . . . yes, I've done it all. Let me advise you. Get a good woman to stick by you. Never mind what the world says. Keep at it. Keep your shoulder to the wheel. It'll pay dividends.

Pause.

[*With a laugh.*] You must excuse my chatting away like this. We have few visitors this time of the year. All our friends summer abroad. I'm a home bird myself. Wouldn't mind taking a trip to Asia Minor, mind you, or to certain lower regions of the Congo, but Europe? Out of the question. Much too noisy. I'm sure you agree. Now look, what will you have to drink? A glass of ale? Curaçao Fockink Orange? Ginger beer? Tia Maria? A Wachenheimer Fuchsmantel Reisling Beeren Auslese? Gin and it? Chateauneuf-du-Pape? A little Asti Spumante? Or what do you say to a straightforward Piesporter Goldtropfschen Feine Auslese (Reichsgraf von Kesselstaff)? Any preference?

[*Pause.*]

You look a trifle warm. Why don't you take off your balaclava? I'd find that a little itchy myself. But then I've always been one for freedom of movement. Even in the depth of winter I wear next to nothing.

[*Pause.*]

I say, can I ask you a personal question? I don't want to seem inquisitive but aren't you rather on the wrong road for matchselling? Not terribly busy, is it? Of course you may not care for petrol fumes or the noise of traffic. I can quite understand that.

[*Pause.*]

Do forgive me peering but is that a glass eye you're wearing?

[*Pause.*]

Do take off your balaclava, there's a good chap, put your tray down and take your ease, as they say in this part of the world. [*He moves towards him.*] I must say you keep quite a good stock, don't you? Tell me, between ourselves, are those boxes full, or are there just a few half-empty ones among them? Oh yes, I used to be in commerce. Well now, before the good lady sounds the gong for petit déjeuner will you join me in an apéritif? I recommend a glass of cider. Now . . . just a minute . . . I know I've got some—Look out! Mind your tray!

The tray falls, and the matchboxes.

Good God, what . . . ?

[*Pause.*]
You've dropped your tray.

Pause. He picks the matchboxes up.

[*Grunts.*] Eh, these boxes are all wet. You've no right to
sell wet matches, you know. Uuuuugggh. This feels sus-
piciously like fungus. You won't get very far in this trade
if you don't take care of your goods. [*Grunts, rising.*] Well,
here you are.
[*Pause.*]
Here's your tray.

He puts the tray into the MATCHSELLER'S *hands, and sits.
Pause.*

Now listen, let me be quite frank with you, shall I? I
really cannot understand why you don't sit down. There
are four chairs at your disposal. Not to mention the hassock.
I can't possibly talk to you unless you're settled. Then and
only then can I speak to you. Do you follow me? You're
not being terribly helpful. [*Slight pause.*] You're sweating.
The sweat's pouring out of you. Take off that balaclava.
[*Pause.*]
Go into the corner then. Into the corner. Go on. Get into
the shade of the corner. Back. Backward.
[*Pause.*]
Get back!
[*Pause.*]
Ah, you understand me. Forgive me for saying so, but I
had decided that you had the comprehension of a bullock.
I was mistaken. You understand me perfectly well. That's
right. A little more. A little to the right. Aaah. Now you're
there. In shade, in shadow. Good-o. Now I can get down
to brass tacks. Can't I?
[*Pause.*]

No doubt you're wondering why I invited you into this house? You may think I was alarmed by the look of you. You would be quite mistaken. I was not alarmed by the look of you. I did not find you at all alarming. No, no. Nothing outside this room has ever alarmed me. You disgusted me, quite forcibly, if you want to know the truth. [*Pause.*]
Why did you disgust me to that extent? That seems to be a pertinent question. You're no more disgusting than Fanny, the squire's daughter, after all. In appearance you differ but not in essence. There's the same . . .
[*Pause.*]
The same . . .
[*Pause.*]
[*In a low voice.*] I want to ask you a question. Why do you stand outside my back gate, from dawn till dusk, why do you pretend to sell matches, why . . . ? What is it, damn you. You're shivering. You're sagging. Come here, come here . . . mind your tray! [EDWARD *rises and moves behind a chair.*] Come, quick quick. There. Sit here. Sit . . . sit in this.

The MATCHSELLER *stumbles and sits. Pause.*

Aaaah! You're sat. At last. What a relief. You must be tired. [*Slight pause.*] Chair comfortable? I bought it in a sale. I bought all the furniture in this house in a sale. The same sale. When I was a young man. You too, perhaps. You too, perhaps.
[*Pause.*]
At the same time, perhaps!
[*Pause.*]
[*Muttering.*] I must get some air. I must get a breath of air.

He goes to the door.

Flora!

FLORA: Yes?

EDWARD [*with great weariness*]: Take me into the garden.

Silence. They move from the study door to a chair under a canopy.

FLORA: Come under the canopy.

EDWARD: Ah. [*He sits.*]

[*Pause.*]

The peace. The peace out here.

FLORA: Look at our trees.

EDWARD: Yes.

FLORA: Our own trees. Can you hear the birds?

EDWARD: No, I can't hear them.

FLORA: But they're singing, high up, and flapping.

EDWARD: Good. Let them flap.

FLORA: Shall I bring your lunch out here? You can have it in peace, and a quiet drink, under your canopy.

[*Pause.*]

How are you getting on with your old man?

EDWARD: What do you mean?

FLORA: What's happening? How are you getting on with him?

EDWARD: Very well. We get on remarkably well. He's a little . . . reticent. Somewhat withdrawn. It's understandable. I should be the same, perhaps, in his place. Though, of course, I could not possibly find myself in his place.

FLORA: Have you found out anything about him?

EDWARD: A little. A little. He's had various trades, that's certain. His place of residence is unsure. He's . . . he's not a drinking man. As yet, I haven't discovered the reason for his arrival here. I shall in due course . . . by nightfall.

FLORA: Is it necessary?

EDWARD: Necessary?

FLORA [*quickly sitting on the right arm of the chair*]: I could show him out now, it wouldn't matter. You've seen him, he's harmless, unfortunate . . . old, that's all. Edward—

listen—he's not here through any . . . design, or anything, I know it. I mean, he might just as well stand outside our back gate as anywhere else. He'll move on. I can . . . make him. I promise you. There's no point in upsetting yourself like this. He's an old man, weak in the head . . . that's all. [*Pause.*]

EDWARD: You're deluded.

FLORA: Edward—

EDWARD [*rising*]: You're deluded. And stop calling me Edward.

FLORA: You're not still frightened of him?

EDWARD: Frightened of him? Of *him*? Have you *seen* him? [*Pause.*] He's like jelly. A great bullockfat of jelly. He can't see straight. I think as a matter of fact he wears a glass eye. He's almost stone deaf . . . almost . . . not quite. He's very nearly dead on his feet. Why should he frighten me? No, you're a woman, you know nothing. [*Slight pause.*] But he possesses other faculties. Cunning. The man's an imposter and he knows I know it.

FLORA: I'll tell you what. Look. Let me speak to him. I'll speak to him.

EDWARD [*quietly*]: And I know he knows I know it.

FLORA: I'll find out all about him, Edward. I promise you I will.

EDWARD: And he knows I know.

FLORA: Edward! Listen to me! I can find out all about him, I promise you. I shall go and have a word with him now. I shall . . . get to the bottom of it.

EDWARD: You? It's laughable.

FLORA: You'll see—he won't bargain for me. I'll surprise him. He'll . . . he'll admit everything.

EDWARD [*softly*]: He'll admit everything, will he?

FLORA: You wait and see, you just—

EDWARD [*hissing*]: What are you plotting?

FLORA: I know exactly what I shall—

EDWARD: What are you plotting?

He seizes her arms.

FLORA: Edward, you're hurting me!
[*Pause.*]
[*With dignity.*] I shall wave from the window when I'm
ready. Then you can come up. I shall get to the truth of it,
I assure you. You're much too heavy-handed, in every way.
You should trust your wife more, Edward. You should trust
her judgment, and have a greater insight into her capa-
bilities. A woman . . . a woman will often succeed, you
know, where a man must invariably fail.

Silence. She goes into the study.

Do you mind if I come in?

The door closes.

Are you comfortable?
[*Pause.*]
Oh, the sun's shining directly on you. Wouldn't you rather
sit in the shade?

She sits down.

It's the longest day of the year today, did you know that?
Actually the year has flown. I can remember Christmas
and that dreadful frost. And the floods! I hope you weren't
here in the floods. We were out of danger up here, of course,
but in the valleys whole families I remember drifted away
on the current. The country was a lake. Everything stopped.
We lived on our own preserves, drank elderberry wine,
studied other cultures.
[*Pause.*]
Do you know, I've got a feeling I've seen you before,
somewhere. Long before the flood. You were much younger.
Yes, I'm really sure of it. Between ourselves, were you ever

a poacher? I had an encounter with a poacher once. It was
a ghastly rape, the brute. High up on a hillside cattle track.
Early spring. I was out riding on my pony. And there on the
verge a man lay—ostensibly injured, lying on his front, I
remember, possibly the victim of a murderous assault, how
was I to know? I dismounted, I went to him, he rose, I
fell, my pony took off, down to the valley. I saw the sky
through the trees, blue. Up to my ears in mud. It was a
desperate battle.

[*Pause.*]

I lost.

[*Pause.*]

Of course, life was perilous in those days. It was my first
canter unchaperoned.

[*Pause.*]

Years later, when I was a Justice of the Peace for the county,
I had him in front of the bench. He was there for poaching.
That's how I know he was a poacher. The evidence though
was sparse, inadmissible, I acquitted him, letting him off
with a caution. He'd grown a red beard, I remember. Yes.
A bit of a stinker.

[*Pause.*]

I say, you are perspiring, aren't you? Shall I mop your
brow? With my chiffon? Is it the heat? Or the closeness?
Or confined space? Or . . .? [*She goes over to him.*]
Actually, the day is cooling. It'll soon be dusk. Perhaps it
is dusk. May I? You don't mind?

[*Pause. She mops his brow.*]

Ah, there, that's better. And your cheeks. It is a woman's
job, isn't it? And I'm the only woman on hand. There.

Pause. She leans on the arm of chair.

[*Intimately.*] Tell me, have you a woman? Do you like
women? Do you ever . . . think about women?

[*Pause.*]

Have you ever . . . stopped a woman?
[*Pause.*]
I'm sure you must have been quite attractive once. [*She sits.*] Not any more, of course. You've got a vile smell. Vile. Quite repellent, in fact.
[*Pause.*]
Sex, I suppose, means nothing to you. Does it ever occur to you that sex is a very vital experience for other people? Really, I think you'd amuse me if you weren't so hideous. You're probably quite amusing in your own way. [*Seductively.*] Tell me all about love. Speak to me of love.
[*Pause.*]
God knows what you're saying at this very moment. It's quite disgusting. Do you know when I was a girl I loved . . . I loved . . . I simply adored . . . what *have* you got on, for goodness sake? A jersey? It's clogged. Have you been rolling in mud? [*Slight pause.*] You haven't been rolling in mud, have you? [*She rises and goes over to him.*] And what have you got under your jersey? Let's see. [*Slight pause.*] I'm not tickling you, am I? No. Good . . . Lord, is this a vest? That's quite original. Quite original. [*She sits on the arm of his chair.*] Hmmnn, you're a solid old boy, I must say. Not at all like a jelly. All you need is a bath. A lovely lathery bath. And a good scrub. A lovely lathery scrub. [*Pause.*] Don't you? It will be a pleasure. [*She throws her arms round him.*] I'm going to keep you. I'm going to keep you, you dreadful chap, and call you Barnabas. Isn't it dark, Barnabas? Your eyes, your eyes, your great big eyes.

Pause.

My husband would never have guessed your name. Never. [*She kneels at his feet. Whispering.*] It's me you were waiting for, wasn't it? You've been standing waiting for me. You've seen me in the woods, picking daisies, in my apron, my pretty daisy apron, and you came and stood, poor creature, at my gate, till death us do part. Poor Barnabas. I'm going to put you to bed. I'm going to put you to bed and watch over you. But first you must have a good whacking great bath. And I'll buy you pretty little things that will suit you. And little toys to play with. On your deathbed. Why shouldn't you die happy?

A shout from the hall.

EDWARD: Well?

[*Footsteps upstage.*]

Well?

FLORA: Don't come in.

EDWARD: Well?

FLORA: He's dying.

EDWARD: Dying? He's not dying.

FLORA: I tell you, he's very ill.

EDWARD: He's not dying! Nowhere near. He'll see you cremated.

FLORA: The man is desperately ill!

EDWARD: Ill? You lying slut. Get back to your trough!

FLORA: Edward . . .

EDWARD [*violently*]: To your trough!

She goes out. Pause.

[*Coolly.*] Good evening to you. Why are you sitting in the gloom? Oh, you've begun to disrobe. Too warm? Let's open these windows, then, what?

He opens the windows.

Pull the blinds.

He pulls the blinds.

And close . . . the curtains . . . again.

He closes the curtains.

Ah. Air will enter through the side chinks. Of the blinds. And filter through the curtains. I hope. Don't want to suffocate, do we?

[*Pause.*]

More comfortable? Yes. You look different in darkness. Take off all your togs, if you like. Make yourself at home. Strip to your buff. Do as you would in your own house.

[*Pause.*]

Did you say something?

[*Pause.*]

Did you say something?

[*Pause.*]

Anything? Well then, tell me about your boyhood. Mmnn?

[*Pause.*]

What did you do with it? Run? Swim? Kick the ball? You kicked the ball? What position? Left back? Goalie? First reserve?

[*Pause.*]

I used to play myself. Country house matches, mostly. Kept wicket and batted number seven.

[*Pause.*]

Kept wicket and batted number seven. Man called—Cavendish, I think had something of your style. Bowled left arm over the wicket, always kept his cap on, quite a dab hand at solo whist, preferred a good round of prop and cop to anything else.

[*Pause.*]

On wet days when the field was swamped.

[*Pause.*]

Perhaps you don't play cricket.

[*Pause.*]

Perhaps you never met Cavendish and never played cricket. You look less and less like a cricketer the more I see of you. Where did you live in those days? God damn it, I'm entitled to know something about you! You're in my blasted

house, on my territory, drinking my wine, eating my duck!
Now you've had your fill you sit like a hump, a mouldering
heap. In my room. My den. I can rem . . . [*He stops
abruptly.*]
[*Pause.*]
You find that funny? Are you grinning?
[*Pause.*]
[*In disgust.*] Good Christ, is that a grin on your face?
[*Further disgust.*] It's lopsided. It's all—down on one side.
You're grinning. It amuses you, does it? When I tell you
how well I remember this room, how well I remember
this den. [*Muttering.*] Ha. Yesterday now, it was clear,
clearly defined, so clearly.
[*Pause.*]
The garden, too, was sharp, lucid, in the rain, in the sun.
[*Pause.*]
My den, too, was sharp, arranged for my purpose . . .
quite satisfactory.
[*Pause.*]
The house too, was polished, all the banisters were polished,
and the stair rods, and the curtain rods.
[*Pause.*]
My desk was polished, and my cabinet.
[*Pause.*]
I was polished. [*Nostalgic.*] I could stand on the hill and
look through my telescope at the sea. And follow the path
of the three-masted schooner, feeling fit, well aware of my
sinews, their suppleness, my arms lifted holding the
telescope, steady, easily, no trembling, my aim was perfect,
I could pour hot water down the spoon-hole, yes, easily, no
difficulty, my grasp firm, my command established, my
life was accounted for, I was ready for my excursions to the
cliff, down the path to the back gate, through the long
grass, no need to watch for the nettles, my progress was
fluent, after my long struggling against all kinds of usurpers,

disreputables, lists, literally lists of people anxious to do me down, and my reputation down, my command was established, all summer I would breakfast, survey my landscape, take my telescope, examine the overhanging of my hedges, pursue the narrow lane past the monastery, climb the hill, adjust the lens [*he mimes a telescope*], watch the progress of the three-masted schooner, my progress was as sure, as fluent . . .

Pause. He drops his arms.

Yes, yes, you're quite right, it is funny.
[*Pause.*]
Laugh your bloody head off! Go on. Don't mind me. No need to be polite.
[*Pause.*]
That's right.
[*Pause.*]
You're quite right, it is funny. I'll laugh with you!

He laughs.

Ha-ha-ha! Yes! You're laughing with me, I'm laughing with you, we're laughing together!

He laughs and stops.

[*Brightly.*] Why did I invite you into this room? That's your next question, isn't it? Bound to be.
[*Pause.*]
Well, why not, you might say? My oldest acquaintance. My nearest and dearest. My kith and kin. But surely correspondence would have been as satisfactory . . . more satisfactory? We could have exchanged postcards, couldn't we? What? Views, couldn't we? Of sea and land, city and village, town and country, autumn and winter . . . clocktowers . . . museums . . . citadels . . . bridges . . . rivers . . .

[*Pause.*]

Seeing you stand, at the back gate, such close proximity, was not at all the same thing.

[*Pause.*]

What are you doing? You're taking off your balaclava . . . you've decided not to. No, very well then, all things considered, did I then invite you into this room with express intention of asking you to take off your balaclava, in order to determine your resemblance to—some other person? The answer is no, certainly not, I did not, for when I first saw you you wore no balaclava. No headcovering of any kind, in fact. You looked quite different without a head—I mean without a hat—I mean without a headcovering, of any kind. In fact every time I have seen you you have looked quite different to the time before.

[*Pause.*]

Even now you look different. Very different.

[*Pause.*]

Admitted that sometimes I viewed you through dark glasses, yes, and sometimes through light glasses, and on other occasions bare eyed, and on other occasions through the bars of the scullery window, or from the roof, the roof, yes in driving snow, or from the bottom of the drive in thick fog, or from the roof again in blinding sun, so blinding, so hot, that I had to skip and jump and bounce in order to remain in one place. Ah, that's good for a guffaw, is it? That's good for a belly laugh? Go on, then. Let it out. Let yourself go, for God's . . . [*He catches his breath.*] You're crying . . .

[*Pause.*]

[*Moved.*] You haven't been laughing. You're crying.

[*Pause.*]

You're weeping. You're shaking with grief. For me. I can't believe it. For my plight. I've been wrong.

[*Pause.*]

[*Briskly.*] Come, come, stop it. Be a man. Blow your nose for goodness sake. Pull yourself together.

He sneezes.

Ah.

He rises. Sneeze.

Ah. Fever. Excuse me.

He blows his nose.

I've caught a cold. A germ. In my eyes. It was this morning. In my eyes. My eyes.

Pause. He falls to the floor.

Not that I had any difficulty in seeing you, no, no, it was not so much my sight, my sight is excellent—in winter I run about with nothing on but a pair of polo shorts—no, it was not so much any deficiency in my sight as the airs between me and my object—don't weep—the change of air, the currents obtaining in the space between me and my object, the shades they make, the shapes they take, the quivering, the eternal quivering—please stop crying—nothing to do with heat-haze. Sometimes, of course, I would take shelter, shelter to compose myself. Yes, I would seek a tree, a cranny of bushes, erect my canopy and so make shelter. And rest. [*Low murmur.*] And then I no longer heard the wind or saw the sun. Nothing entered, nothing left my nook. I lay on my side in my polo shorts, my fingers lightly in contact with the blades of grass, the earthflowers, the petals of the earth-flowers flaking, lying on my palm, the underside of all the great foliage dark, above me, but it is only afterwards I say the foliage was dark, the petals flaking, then I said nothing, I remarked nothing, things happened upon me, then in my times of shelter, the shades, the petals, carried themselves, carried their bodies upon me, and nothing entered my nook, nothing left it.

[*Pause.*]
But then, the time came. I saw the wind. I saw the wind, swirling, and the dust at my back gate, lifting, and the long grass, scything together . . . [*Slowly, in horror.*] You *are* laughing. You're laughing. Your face. Your body. [*Overwhelming nausea and horror.*] Rocking . . . gasping . . . rocking . . . shaking . . . rocking . . . heaving . . . rocking . . . You're laughing at me! Aaaaahhhh!

The MATCHSELLER *rises. Silence.*

You look younger. You look extraordinarily . . . youthful. [*Pause.*]
You want to examine the garden? It must be very bright, in the moonlight. [*Becoming weaker.*] I would like to join you . . . explain . . . show you . . . the garden . . . explain . . . The plants . . . where I run . . . my track . . . in training . . . I was number one sprinter at Howells . . . when a stripling . . . no more than a stripling . . . licked . . . men twice my strength . . . when a stripling . . . like yourself.
[*Pause.*]
[*Flatly.*] The pool must be glistening. In the moonlight. And the lawn. I remember it well. The cliff. The sea. The three-masted schooner.
[*Pause.*]
[*With great, final effort—a whisper.*] Who are you?
FLORA [*off*]: Barnabas?
[*Pause.*]

She enters.

Ah, Barnabas. Everything is ready.
[*Pause.*]
I want to show you my garden, your garden. You must see my japonica, my convolvulus . . . my honeysuckle, my clematis.

[*Pause.*]

The summer is coming. I've put up your canopy for you. You can lunch in the garden, by the pool. I've polished the whole house for you.

[*Pause.*]

Take my hand.

Pause. The MATCHSELLER *goes over to her.*

Yes. Oh, wait a moment.

[*Pause.*]

Edward. Here is your tray.

She crosses to EDWARD *with the tray of matches, and puts it in his hands. Then she and the* MATCHSELLER *start to go out as the curtain falls slowly.*

The Collection

The Collection was first presented by Associated-Rediffusion Television, London, on 11 May 1961, with the following cast:

HARRY, *a man in his forties*   Griffith Jones
JAMES, *a man in his thirties*   Anthony Bate
STELLA, *a woman in her thirties*   Vivien Merchant
BILL, *a man in his late twenties*   John Ronane

Directed by Joan Kemp-Welch

It was presented by the Royal Shakespeare Company at the Aldwych Theatre, London, on 18 June 1962, with the following cast:

HARRY   Michael Horden
JAMES   Kenneth Haigh
STELLA   Barbara Murray
BILL   John Ronane

Directed by Peter Hall and Harold Pinter

The stage is divided into three areas, two peninsulas and a promontory. Each area is distinct and separate from the other.

Stage left Harry's house, in Belgravia. Elegant decor. Period furnishing. This set comprises the living-room, hall, front door and staircase to first floor. Kitchen exit below staircase.

Stage right James' flat, in Chelsea. Tasteful contemporary furnishing. This set comprises the living-room only. Off stage right other rooms and front door.

Up stage centre on promontory telephone box.

The Collection

The telephone box is lit in a half light. A figure can be dimly observed inside it, with his back to the audience. The rest of the stage is dark. In the house the telephone is ringing. It is late at night.

Night light in house fades up. Street fades up.

HARRY *approaches the house, opens the front door and goes in. He switches on a light in the hall, goes into the living-room, walks to the telephone and lifts it.*

HARRY: Hullo.

VOICE: Is that you, Bill?

HARRY: No, he's in bed. Who's this?

VOICE: In bed?

HARRY: Who is this?

VOICE: What's he doing in bed?

Pause.

HARRY: Do you know it's four o'clock in the morning?

VOICE: Well, give him a nudge. Tell him I want a word with him.

Pause.

HARRY: Who is this?

VOICE: Go and wake him up, there's a good boy.

Pause.

HARRY: Are you a friend of his?

VOICE: He'll know me when he sees me.

HARRY: Oh yes?

Pause.

VOICE: Aren't you going to wake him?
HARRY: No, I'm not.

Pause.

VOICE: Tell him I'll be in touch.

The telephone cuts off. HARRY *replaces the receiver and stands still. The figure leaves the telephone box.* HARRY *walks slowly into hall, switches off the light, walks up the stairs.*
Fade to blackout.
Fade up on flat. It is morning.
JAMES, *smoking, enters, sits on sofa.* STELLA *enters from bedroom fixing bracelet on her wrist. She goes to cabinet, takes a perfume atomizer from her handbag and uses it on her throat and hands. She puts the atomizer into her bag and begins to put her gloves on.*

STELLA: I'm going.

Pause.

Aren't you coming in today?

Pause.

JAMES: No.
STELLA: You had to meet those people from . . .

Pause. She slowly walks to an armchair, picks up her jacket, puts it on.

You had to meet those people about that order.
Shall I phone them when I get to the shop?
JAMES: You could do . . . yes.
STELLA: What are you going to do?

He looks at her, with a brief smile, then away.

Jimmy . . .

Pause.

Are you going out?

Pause.

Will you . . . be in tonight?

JAMES *reaches for a glass ashtray, flicks ash, regards the ash-tray.* STELLA *turns, leaves the room. The front door slams.*
JAMES *continues regarding the ashtray.*
Fade to half light.
Fade up on house. Morning.
BILL *brings on tray from kitchen and places it on the table, arranges it, pours tea, sits, picks up newspaper, reads, drinks.*
HARRY, *in dressing gown, descends stairs, trips, stumbles.*

BILL [*turning*]: What have you done?
HARRY: I tripped on that stair rod!

He comes into the room.

BILL: All right?
HARRY: It's that stair rod. I thought you said you were going to fix it.
BILL: I did fix it.
HARRY: Well, you didn't fix it very well.

He sits, holding his head.

Ooh.

BILL *pours tea for him.*
In the flat, JAMES *stubs his cigarette and goes out. The lights in the flat fade out.*
HARRY *sips the tea, puts cup down.*

HARRY: Where's my fruit juice? I haven't had my fruit juice.

BILL *regards fruit juice on tray.*

What's it doing over there?

BILL *gives it to him.* HARRY *sips it.*

What's this? Pineapple?

BILL: Grapefruit.

Pause.

HARRY: I'm sick and tired of that stair rod. Why don't you screw it in or something? You're supposed ... you're supposed to be able to use your hands.

Pause.

BILL: What time did you get in?

HARRY: Four.

BILL: Good party?

Pause.

HARRY: You didn't make any toast this morning.

BILL: No. Do you want some?

HARRY: No. I don't.

BILL: I can if you like.

HARRY: It's all right. Don't bother.

Pause.

How are you spending your day today?

BILL: Go and see a film, I think.

HARRY: Wonderful life you lead.

Pause.

Do you know some maniac telephoned you last night?

BILL *looks at him.*

Just as I got in. Four o'clock. Walked in the door and the telephone was ringing.

BILL: Who was it?

HARRY: I've no idea.

BILL: What did he want?

HARRY: You. He was shy, wouldn't tell me his name.

BILL: Huh.

Pause.

HARRY: Who could it have been?

BILL: I've no idea.

HARRY: He was very insistent. Said he was going to get in touch again.

Pause.

Who the hell was it?

BILL: I've just said . . . I haven't the remotest idea.

Pause.

HARRY: Did you meet anyone last week?

BILL: Meet anyone? What do you mean?

HARRY: I mean could it have been anyone you met? You must have met lots of people.

BILL: I didn't speak to a soul.

HARRY: Must have been miserable for you.

BILL: I was only there one night, wasn't I? Some more?

HARRY: No thank you.

BILL *pours tea for himself.*
The telephone box fades up to half light, disclosing a figure entering it.

I must shave.

HARRY *sits, looking at* BILL, *who is reading the paper. After a moment* BILL *looks up.*

BILL: Mmnnn?

Silence. HARRY *stands, leaves the room and exits up the stairs, treading carefully over the stair rod.* BILL *reads paper. The telephone rings.*
BILL *lifts the receiver.*

BILL: Hullo.
VOICE: Is that you, Bill?
BILL: Yes?
VOICE: Are you in?
BILL: Who's this?
VOICE: Don't move. I'll be straight round.
BILL: What do you mean? Who is this?
VOICE: About two minutes. All right?
BILL: You can't do that. I've got some people here.
VOICE: Never mind. We can go into another room.
BILL: This is ridiculous. Do I know you?
VOICE: You'll know me when you see me.
BILL: Do you know me?
VOICE: Just stay where you are. I'll be right round.
BILL: But what do you want, who—? You can't do that, I'm going straight out, I won't be in.
VOICE: See you.

The phone cuts off. BILL *replaces the receiver.*
The lights on the telephone box fade as the figure comes out and exits left.
BILL *puts on his jacket, goes into the hall, puts on overcoat, swift but not hurried, opens front door and goes out. He exits up right.* HARRY'S *voice from upstairs.*

HARRY: Bill, was that you?

He appears at the head of the stairs.

Bill!

He goes downstairs into living-room, stands, observes tray, takes tray into kitchen.

JAMES *comes from up left in street and looks at the house.*
HARRY *comes out of kitchen, goes into hall and up the stairs.*
JAMES *rings the bell.*
HARRY *comes down the stairs and opens the door.*

HARRY: Yes?
JAMES: I'm looking for Bill Lloyd.
HARRY: He's out. Can I help?
JAMES: When will he be in?
HARRY: I can't say. Does he know you?
JAMES: I'll try some other time then.
HARRY: Well, perhaps you'd like to leave your name. I can tell him when I see him.
JAMES: No, that's all right. Just tell him I called.
HARRY: Tell him who called?
JAMES: Sorry to bother you.
HARRY: Just a minute. [JAMES *turns back.*] You're not the man who telephoned last night, are you?
JAMES: Last night?
HARRY: You didn't telephone early this morning?
JAMES: No . . . sorry . . .
HARRY: Well, what do you want?
JAMES: I'm looking for Bill.
HARRY: You didn't by any chance telephone just now?
JAMES: I think you've got the wrong man.
HARRY: I think you have.
JAMES: I don't think you know anything about it.

JAMES turns, goes. HARRY stands watching him. He closes door, goes towards stairs.
Fade to blackout.
Fade up moonlight in flat.
Front door closes, in flat.
STELLA *comes in, stands, switches on a lamp. She turns in direction of other rooms.*

STELLA: Jimmy?

Silence.
*She takes gloves off, puts handbag down, is still. She goes to
record player, puts on a record. It is Charlie Parker. She
listens, then exits to bedroom.*
Fade up house. Night.
BILL *enters living-room from kitchen with magazines. He
throws them in the hearth, goes to drinks table and pours a
drink, lies on floor with drink by the hearth, flicking through
a magazine.*
STELLA *comes back into room with a white Persian kitten. She
lies back on sofa, nuzzling it.*
HARRY *comes downstairs, glances in at* BILL, *exits, walks down
street to U. R.*
JAMES *appears at front door of house from U. L., looks after*
HARRY, *rings the bell.*
BILL *stands, goes to door.*
Fade flat to half light and music out.

BILL: Yes?
JAMES: Bill Lloyd?
BILL: Yes?
JAMES: Oh, I'd . . . I'd like to have a word with you.

Pause.

BILL: I'm sorry, I don't think I know you?
JAMES: Don't you?
BILL: No.
JAMES: Well there's something I'd like to talk to you
about.
BILL: I'm terribly sorry, I'm busy.
JAMES: It won't take long.
BILL: I'm awfully sorry. Perhaps you'd like to put it down on
paper and send it to me.
JAMES: That's not possible.

Pause.

BILL [*closing door*]: Do forgive me—
JAMES [*foot in door*]: Look. I want to speak to you.

Pause.

BILL: Did you phone me today?
JAMES: That's right. I called, but you'd gone out.
BILL: You called here? I didn't know that.
JAMES: I think I'd better come in, don't you?
BILL: You can't just barge into someone's house like this, you know. What do you want?
JAMES: Why don't you stop wasting your time and let me in?
BILL: I could call the police.
JAMES: Not worth it.

They stare at each other.

BILL: All right.

JAMES *goes in.* BILL *closes the door.* JAMES *goes through hall and into living-room.* BILL *follows.* JAMES *looks about the room.*

JAMES: Got any olives?
BILL: How did you know my name?
JAMES: No olives?
BILL: Olives? I'm afraid not.
JAMES: You mean to say you don't keep olives for your guests?
BILL: You're not my guest, you're an intruder. What can I do for you?
JAMES: Do you mind if I sit down?
BILL: Yes, I do.
JAMES: You'll get over it.

JAMES *sits.* BILL *stands.* JAMES *stands, takes off his overcoat, throws it on an armchair, sits again.*

BILL: What's your name, old boy?

JAMES reaches to a bowl of fruit and breaks off a grape, which he eats.

JAMES: Where shall I put the pips?
BILL: In your wallet.

JAMES takes out his wallet and deposits the pips. He regards BILL.

JAMES: You're not a bad-looking bloke.
BILL: Oh, thanks.
JAMES: You're not a film star, but you're quite tolerable look-ing, I suppose.
BILL: That's more than I can say for you.
JAMES: I'm not interested in what you can say for me.
BILL: To put it quite bluntly, old chap, I'm even less interested than you are. Now look, come on please, what do you want?

JAMES stands, walks to drinks table and stares at the bottles. In the flat, STELLA *rises with kitten and goes off slowly, nuzzling it.*
The flat fades to blackout.
JAMES pours himself a whisky.

BILL: Cheers.
JAMES: Did you have a good time in Leeds last week?
BILL: What?
JAMES: Did you have a good time in Leeds last week?
BILL: Leeds?
JAMES: Did you enjoy yourself?
BILL: What makes you think I was in Leeds?
JAMES: Tell me all about it. See much of the town? Get out to the country at all?
BILL: What are you talking about?

Pause.

JAMES [*with fatigue*]: Aaah. You were down there for the dress collection. You took some of your models.

BILL: Did I?

JAMES: You stayed at the Westbury Hotel.

BILL: Oh?

JAMES: Room 142.

BILL: 142? Oh. Was it comfortable?

JAMES: Comfortable enough.

BILL: Oh, good.

JAMES: Well, you had your yellow pyjamas with you.

BILL: Did I really? What, the ones with the black initials?

JAMES: Yes, you had them on you in 165.

BILL: In what?

JAMES: 165.

BILL: 165? I thought I was in 142.

JAMES: You booked into 142. But you didn't stay there.

BILL: Well, that's a bit silly, isn't it? Booking a room and not staying in it?

JAMES: 165 is just along the passage to 142, you're not far away.

BILL: Oh well, that's a relief.

JAMES: You could easily nip back to shave.

BILL: From 165?

JAMES: Yes.

BILL: What was I doing there?

JAMES [*casually*]: My wife was in there. That's where you slept with her.

Silence.

BILL: Well . . . who told you that?

JAMES: She did.

BILL: You should have her seen to.

JAMES: Be careful.

BILL: Mmmm? Who is your wife?

JAMES: You know her.

BILL: I don't think so.

JAMES: No?

BILL: No, I don't think so at all.

JAMES: I see.

BILL: I was nowhere near Leeds last week, old chap. Nowhere near your wife either, I'm quite sure of that. Apart from that, I . . . just don't do such things. Not in my book.

Pause.

I wouldn't dream of it. Well, I think that closes the subject, don't you?

JAMES: Come here. I want to tell you something.

BILL: I'm expecting guests in a minute, you know. Cocktails, I'm standing for Parliament next season.

JAMES: Come here.

BILL: I'm going to be Minister for Home Affairs.

JAMES *moves to him.*

JAMES [*confidentially*]: When you treat my wife like a whore, then I think I'm entitled to know what you've got to say about it.

BILL: But I don't know your wife.

JAMES: You do. You met her at ten o'clock last Friday in the lounge. You fell into conversation, you bought her a couple of drinks, you went upstairs together in the lift. In the lift you never took your eyes from her, you found you were both on the same floor, you helped her out, by her arm. You stood with her in the corridor, looking at her. You touched her shoulder, said goodnight, went to your room, she went to hers, you changed into your yellow pyjamas and black dressing gown, you went down the passage and knocked on her door, you'd left your toothpaste in town. She opened the door, you went in, she was still dressed. You admired the room, it was so feminine, you felt awake, didn't feel like sleeping, you sat down on the bed. She wanted you to go, you wouldn't. She became upset, you sympathized, away from home, on business, horrible life, especially for a woman, you comforted her, you gave her solace, you stayed.

Pause.

BILL: Look, do you mind . . . just going off now. You're giving me a bit of a headache.

JAMES: You knew she was married . . . why did you feel it necessary . . . to do that?

BILL: She must have known she was married too. Why did she feel it necessary . . . to do that?

Pause.

[*With a chuckle.*] That's got you, hasn't it?

Pause.

Well, look, it's really just a lot of rubbish. You know that.

BILL *goes to cigarette box, lights cigarette.*

Is she supposed to have resisted me at all?

JAMES: A little.

BILL: Only a little?

JAMES: Yes.

BILL: Do you believe her?

JAMES: Yes.

BILL: Everything she says?

JAMES: Sure.

BILL: Did she bite at all?

JAMES: No.

BILL: Scratch?

JAMES: A little.

BILL: You've got a devoted wife, haven't you? Keeps you very well informed, right up to the minutest detail. She scratched a little, did she? Where? [*Holds up hand.*] On the hand?

No scar. No scar anywhere. Absolutely unscarred. We can go before a commissioner of oaths, if you like. I'll strip, show you my unscarred body. Yes, what we need is an independent witness. You got any chambermaids on your side or anything?

JAMES *applauds briefly*.

JAMES: You're a wag, aren't you? I never thought you'd be such a wag. You've really got a sense of fun. You know what I'd call you?

BILL: What?

JAMES: A wag.

BILL: Oh, thanks very much.

JAMES: No, I'm glad to pay a compliment when a compliment's due. What about a drink?

BILL: That's good of you.

JAMES: What will you have?

BILL: Got any vodka?

JAMES: Let's see. Yes, I think we can find you some vodka.

BILL: Oh, scrumptious.

JAMES: Say that again.

BILL: What?

JAMES: That word.

BILL: What, scrumptious?

JAMES: That's it.

BILL: Scrumptious.

JAMES: Marvellous. You probably remember that from school, don't you?

BILL: Now that you mention it I think you might be right.

JAMES: I thought I was. Here's your vodka.

BILL: That's very generous of you.

JAMES: Not at all. Cheers.

BILL: Cheers.

They drink.

JAMES: Eh, come here.

BILL: What?

JAMES: I bet you're a wow at parties.

BILL: Well, it's nice of you to say so, but I wouldn't say I was all that much of a wow.

JAMES: Go on, I bet you are.

Pause.

BILL: You think I'm a wow, do you?

JAMES: At parties I should think you are.

BILL: No, I'm not much of a wow really. The bloke I share this house with is though.

JAMES: Oh, I met him. Looked a jolly kind of chap.

BILL: Yes, he's very good at parties. Bit of a conjurer.

JAMES: What, rabbits?

BILL: Well, not so much rabbits, no.

JAMES: No rabbits?

BILL: No. He doesn't like rabbits, actually. They give him hay fever.

JAMES: Poor chap.

BILL: Yes, it's a pity.

JAMES: Seen a doctor about it?

BILL: Oh, he's had it since he was that high.

JAMES: Brought up in the country, I suppose?

BILL: In a manner of speaking, yes.

Pause.

Ah, well, it's been very nice meeting you, old chap. You must come again when the weather's better.

JAMES *makes a sudden move forward.* BILL *starts back, and falls over a pouffe on to the floor, flat.* JAMES *chuckles.*
Pause.

You've made me spill my drink. You've made me spill it on my cardigan.

JAMES *stands over him.*

I could easily kick you from here.

Pause.

Are you going to let me get up?

Pause.

Are you going to let me get up?

Pause.

Now listen . . . I'll tell you what . . .

Pause.

If you let me get up . . .

Pause.

I'm not very comfortable.

Pause.

If you let me get up . . . I'll . . . I'll tell you . . . the truth . . .

Pause.

JAMES: Tell me the truth from there.
BILL: No. No, when I'm up.
JAMES: Tell me from there.

Pause.

BILL: Oh well, I'm only telling you because I'm utterly bored . . . The truth . . . is that it never happened . . . what you said, anyway. I didn't know she was married. She never told me. Never said a word. But nothing of that . . . happened, I can assure you. All that happened was . . . you were right, actually, about going up in the lift . . .

we . . . got out of the lift, and then suddenly she was in my arms. Really wasn't my fault, nothing was further from my mind, biggest surprise of my life, must have found me terribly attractive quite suddenly, I don't know . . . but I . . . I didn't refuse. Anyway, we just kissed a bit, only a few minutes, by the lift, no one about, and that was that, she went to her room.

He props himself up on pouffe.

The rest of it just didn't happen. I mean, I wouldn't do that sort of thing. I mean, that sort of thing . . . it's just meaningless. I can understand that you're upset, of course, but honestly, there was nothing else to it. Just a few kisses. [*He rises, wiping his cardigan.*] I'm dreadfully sorry, really. I mean, I've no idea why she should make up all that. Pure fantasy. Really rather naughty of her. Rather alarming.

Pause.

Do you know her well?

JAMES: And then about midnight you went into her private bathroom and had a bath. You sang 'Coming through the Rye'. You used her bath towel. Then you walked about the room with her bath towel, pretending you were a Roman.

BILL: Did I?

JAMES: Then I phoned.

Pause.

I spoke to her. Asked her how she was. She said she was all right. Her voice was a little low. I asked her to speak up. She didn't have much to say. You were sitting on the bed, next to her.

Silence.

BILL: Not sitting. Lying.

Blackout.
Church bells.
Full light up on both the flat and the house.
Sunday morning.
JAMES *is sitting alone in the living-room of the flat, reading the paper.*
HARRY *and* BILL *are sitting in the living-room of the house, coffee before them.* BILL *is reading the paper.* HARRY *is watching him.*
Silence.
Church bells.
Silence.

HARRY: Put that paper down.
BILL: What?
HARRY: Put it down.
BILL: Why?
HARRY: You've read it.
BILL: No, I haven't. There's lots to read, you know.
HARRY: I told you to put it down.

BILL *looks at him, throws paper at him, coolly, rises.* HARRY *picks it up and reads.*

BILL: Oh, you just wanted it yourself, did you?
HARRY: Want it? I don't want it.

HARRY *crumples the paper deliberately and drops it.*

I don't want it. Do you want it?

BILL: You're being a little erratic this morning, aren't you?
HARRY: Am I?
BILL: I would say you were.
HARRY: Well, you know what it is, don't you?
BILL: No.
HARRY: It's the church bells. You know how church bells always set me off. You know how they affect me.

BILL: I never hear them.
HARRY: You're not the sort of person who would, are you?
BILL: I'm finding all this faintly idiotic.

   BILL *bends to pick up paper.*

HARRY: Don't touch that paper.
BILL: Why not?
HARRY: Don't touch it.

   BILL *stares at him and then slowly picks it up.*
   Silence.
   He tosses it to HARRY.

BILL: You have it. I don't want it.

   BILL *goes out and up the stairs.* HARRY *opens paper and reads it.*
   In the flat, STELLA *comes in with a tray of coffee and biscuits. She places tray on coffee table, passes a cup to* JAMES. *She sips.*

STELLA: Would you like a biscuit?
JAMES: No, thank you.

   Pause.

STELLA: I'm going to have one.
JAMES: You'll get fat.
STELLA: From biscuits?
JAMES: You don't want to get fat, do you?
STELLA: Why not?
JAMES: Perhaps you do.
STELLA: It's not one of my aims.
JAMES: What is your aim?

   Pause.

   I'd like an olive.
STELLA: Olive? We haven't got any.
JAMES: How do you know?

STELLA: I know.

JAMES: Have you looked?

STELLA: I don't need to look, do I? I know what I've got.

JAMES: You know what you've got?

Pause.

Why haven't we got any olives?

STELLA: I didn't know you liked them.

JAMES: That must be the reason we've never had them in the house. You've simply never been interested enough in olives to ask me whether I liked them or not.

Telephone rings in the house. HARRY *puts paper down and goes to it.* BILL *comes down the stairs. They stop, facing each other, momentarily.* HARRY *lifts receiver.* BILL *walks into room, picks up paper and sits.*

HARRY: Hullo. What? No. Wrong number. [*Replaces receiver.*] Wrong number. Who do you think it was?

BILL: I didn't think.

HARRY: Oh, by the way, a chap called for you yesterday.

BILL: Oh yes?

HARRY: Just after you'd gone out.

BILL: Oh yes?

HARRY: Ah well, time for the joint. Roast or chips?

BILL: I don't want any potatoes, thank you.

HARRY: No potatoes? What an extraordinary thing. Yes, this chap, he was asking for you, he wanted you.

BILL: What for?

HARRY: He wanted to know if you ever cleaned your shoes with furniture polish.

BILL: Really? How odd.

HARRY: Not odd. Some kind of national survey.

BILL: What did he look like?

HARRY: Oh . . . lemon hair, nigger brown teeth, wooden leg, bottlegreen eyes and a toupee. Know him?

BILL: Never met him.

HARRY: You'd know him if you saw him.

BILL: I doubt it.

HARRY: What, a man who looked like that?

BILL: Plenty of men look like that.

HARRY: That's true. That's very true. The only thing is that this particular man was here last night.

BILL: Was he? I didn't see him.

HARRY: Oh yes, he was here, but I've got a funny feeling he wore a mask. It was the same man but he wore a mask, that's all there is to it. He didn't dance here last night, did he, or do any gymnastics?

BILL: No one danced here last night.

HARRY: Aah. Well, that's why you didn't notice his wooden leg. I couldn't help seeing it myself when he came to the front door because he stood on the top step stark naked. Didn't seem very cold though. He had a waterbottle under his arm instead of a hat.

BILL: Those church bells have certainly left their mark on you.

HARRY: They haven't helped, but the fact of the matter is, old chap, that I don't like strangers coming into my house without an invitation.

Pause.

Who is this man and what does he want?

Pause. BILL *rises.*

BILL: Will you excuse me? I really think it's about time I was dressed, don't you?

BILL *goes up the stairs.*
HARRY, *after a moment, turns and follows. He slowly ascends the stairs.*
Fade to blackout on house.

In the flat JAMES *is still reading the paper.* STELLA *is sitting silently.*
Silence.

STELLA: What do you think about going for a run today . . . in the country.

Pause. JAMES *puts the paper down.*

JAMES: I've come to a decision.
STELLA: What?
JAMES: I'm going to go and see him.
STELLA: See him? Who?

Pause.

What for?
JAMES: Oh . . . have a chat with him.
STELLA: What's the point of doing that?
JAMES: I feel I'd like to.
STELLA: I just don't see . . . what there is to be gained. What's the point of it?

Pause.

What are you going to do, hit him?
JAMES: No, no. I'd just like to hear what he's got to say.
STELLA: Why?
JAMES: I want to know what his attitude is.

Pause.

STELLA: He doesn't matter.
JAMES: What do you mean?
STELLA: He's not important.
JAMES: Do you mean anyone would have done? You mean it just happened to be him, but it might as well have been anyone?
STELLA: No.
JAMES: What then?

STELLA: Of course it couldn't have been anyone. It was him. It was just . . . something . . .

JAMES: That's what I mean. It was him. That's why I think he's worth having a look at. I want to see what he's like. It'll be instructive, educational.

Pause.

STELLA: Please don't go and see him. You don't know where he lives, anyway.

JAMES: You don't think I should see him?

STELLA: It won't . . . make you feel any better.

JAMES: I want to see if he's changed.

STELLA: What do you mean?

JAMES: I want to see if he's changed from when I last saw him. He may have gone down the drain since I last saw him. I must say he looked in good shape though.

STELLA: You've never seen him.

Pause.

You don't know him.

Pause.

You don't know where he lives.

Pause.

When did you see him?

JAMES: We had dinner together last night.

STELLA: What?

JAMES: Splendid host.

STELLA: I don't believe it.

JAMES: Ever been to his place?

Pause.

Rather nice. Ever been there?

STELLA: I met him in Leeds, that's all.

JAMES: Oh, is that all. Well, we'll have to go round there one night. The grub's good, I can't deny it. I found him quite charming.

Pause.

He remembered the occasion well. He was perfectly frank. You know, a man's man. Straight from the shoulder. He entirely confirmed your story.

STELLA: Did he?

JAMES: Mmm. Only thing . . . he rather implied that you led him on. Typical masculine thing to say, of course.

STELLA: That's a lie.

JAMES: You know what men are. I reminded him that you'd resisted, that you'd hated the whole thing, but that you'd been—how can we say—somehow hypnotized by him, it happens sometimes. He agreed it can happen sometimes. He told me he'd been hypnotized once by a cat. Wouldn't go into any more details though. Still, I must admit we rather hit it off. We've got the same interests. He was most amusing over the brandy.

STELLA: I'm not interested.

JAMES: In fact, he was most amusing over the whole thing.

STELLA: Was he?

JAMES: But especially over the brandy. He's got the right attitude, you see. As a man, I can only admire it.

STELLA: What is his attitude?

JAMES: What's your attitude?

STELLA: I don't know what you're . . . I just don't know what you're . . . I just . . . hoped you'd understand . . .

She covers her face, crying.

JAMES: Well I do understand, but only after meeting him. Now I'm perfectly happy. I can see it both ways, three ways, all ways . . . every way. It's perfectly clear, there's nothing to it, everything's back to normal. The only difference is that I've come across a man I can respect. It isn't often you can do that, that that happens, and really I suppose I've got you to thank.

He bends forward and pats her arm.

Thanks.

Pause.

He reminds me of a bloke I went to school with. Hawkins. Honestly, he reminded me of Hawkins. Hawkins was an opera fan too. So's whatsisname. I'm a bit of an opera fan myself. Always kept it a dead secret. I might go along with your bloke to the opera one night. He says he can always get free seats. He knows quite a few of that crowd. Maybe I can track old Hawkins down and take him along too. He's a very cultivated bloke, your bloke, quite a considerable intelligence at work there, I thought. He's got a collection of Chinese pots stuck on a wall, must have cost at least 1500 a piece. Well, you can't help noticing that sort of thing. I mean, you couldn't say he wasn't a man of taste. He's brimming over with it. Well, I suppose he must have struck you the same way. No, really, I think I should thank you, rather than anything else. After two years of marriage it looks as though, by accident, you've opened up a whole new world for me.

Fade up house. Night.
BILL *comes in from kitchen with a tray of olives, cheese, crisps, and a transistor radio, playing Vivaldi very quietly. He puts tray on table, arranges cushions, eats a crisp.*
JAMES *appears at the front door and rings the bell.* BILL *goes to door, opens it,* JAMES *comes in. In the hall he helps* JAMES *off with coat.* JAMES *comes into room,* BILL *follows.* JAMES *notices tray with olives, smiles.* BILL *smiles.* JAMES *goes up to Chinese vases, examines them.* BILL *pours drinks.*

In the flat the telephone rings.
Fade up on flat. Night.
A figure can be dimly seen in the telephone box.
STELLA *enters from bedroom, holding kitten. She goes to telephone.*
BILL *gives* JAMES *a glass. They drink.*

STELLA: Hullo.
HARRY: Is that you, James?
STELLA: What? No, it isn't. Who's this?
HARRY: Where's James?
STELLA: He's out.
HARRY: Out? Oh, well, all right. I'll be straight round.
STELLA: What are you talking about? Who are you?
HARRY: Don't go out.

The telephone cuts off. STELLA *replaces receiver, sits upright with kitten on chair.*
Fade to half light on flat.
Fade telephone box.

JAMES: You know something? You remind me of a chap I knew once. Hawkins. Yes. He was quite a tall lad.
BILL: Tall, was he?
JAMES: Yes.
BILL: Now why would I remind you of him?
JAMES: He was quite a card.

Pause.

BILL: Tall, was he?
JAMES: That's . . . what he was.
BILL: Well, you're not short.
JAMES: I'm not tall.
BILL: Quite broad.
JAMES: That doesn't make me tall.
BILL: I never said it did.
JAMES: Well, what are you saying?

BILL: Nothing.

Pause.

JAMES: I wouldn't exactly say I was broad, either.

BILL: Well, you only see yourself in the mirror, don't you?

JAMES: That's good enough for me.

BILL: They're deceptive.

JAMES: Mirrors?

BILL: Very.

JAMES: Have you got one?

BILL: What?

JAMES: A mirror.

BILL: There's one right in front of you.

JAMES: So there is.

JAMES *looks into the mirror.*

Come here. You look in it too.

BILL *stands by him and looks. They look together, and then* JAMES *walks to the left of the mirror and looks again at* BILL'S *reflection.*

I don't think mirrors are deceptive.

JAMES *sits.* BILL *smiles, sits, turns up radio. They sit listening. Fade to half light on house and radio out. Fade up full on flat. Doorbell.* STELLA *rises, goes off to front door. The voices are heard off.*

STELLA: Yes?

HARRY: How do you do. My name's Harry Kane. I wonder if I might have a word with you. There's no need to be alarmed. May I come in?

STELLA: Yes.

HARRY [*entering*]: In here?
STELLA: Yes.

They come into the room.

HARRY: What a beautiful lamp.
STELLA: What can I do for you?
HARRY: Do you know Bill Lloyd?
STELLA: No.
HARRY: Oh, you don't?
STELLA: No.
HARRY: You don't know him personally?
STELLA: I don't, no.
HARRY: I found him in a slum, you know, by accident. Just happened to be in a slum one day and there he was. I realized he had talent straight away. I gave him a roof, gave him a job and he came up trumps. We've been close friends for years.
STELLA: Oh yes?
HARRY: You know of him, of course, don't you, by repute? He's a dress designer.
STELLA: I know of him.
HARRY: You're both dress designers.
STELLA: Yes.
HARRY: You don't belong to the Rags and Bags Club, do you?
STELLA: The what?
HARRY: The Rags and Bags Club. I thought I might have seen you down there.
STELLA: No, I don't know it.
HARRY: Shame. You'd like it.

Pause.

Yes.

Pause.

I've come about your husband.

STELLA: Oh?

HARRY: Yes. He's been bothering Bill recently, with some fantastic story.

STELLA: I know about it. I'm very sorry.

HARRY: Oh, you know? Well, it's really been rather disturbing. I mean, the boy has his work to get on with. This sort of thing spoils his concentration.

STELLA: I'm sorry. It's . . . very unfortunate.

HARRY: It is.

Pause.

STELLA: I can't understand it . . . We've been happily married for two years, you see. I've . . . been away before, you know . . . showing dresses, here and there, my husband runs the business. But it's never happened before.

HARRY: What hasn't?

STELLA: Well, that my husband has suddenly dreamed up such a fantastic story, for no reason at all.

HARRY: That's what I said it was. I said it was a fantastic story.

STELLA: It is.

HARRY: That's what I said and that's what Bill says. We both think it's a fantastic story.

STELLA: I mean, Mr. Lloyd was in Leeds, but I hardly saw him, even though we were staying in the same hotel. I never met him or spoke to him . . . and then my husband suddenly accused me of . . . it's really been very distressing.

HARRY: Yes. What do you think the answer is? Do you think your husband . . . doesn't trust you, or something?

STELLA: Of course he does—he's just not been very well lately, actually . . . overwork.

HARRY: That's bad. Still, you know what it's like in our business. Why don't you take him on a long holiday? South of France.

STELLA: Yes. I'm very sorry that Mr. Lloyd has had to put up with all this, anyway.

HARRY: Oh, what a beautiful kitten, what a really beautiful kitten. Kitty, kitty, kitty, what do you call her, come here kitty, kitty.

HARRY sits next to STELLA and proceeds to pet and nuzzle the kitten.
Fade flat to half light.
Fade up full on house.
BILL and JAMES, with drinks in same position. Music comes up.
BILL turns off radio. Music out.

BILL: Hungry?

JAMES: No.

BILL: Biscuit?

JAMES: I'm not hungry.

BILL: I've got some olives.

JAMES: Really?

BILL: Like one?

JAMES: No thanks.

BILL: Why not?

JAMES: I don't like them.

Pause.

BILL: Don't like olives?

Pause.

What on earth have you got against olives?

JAMES: I detest them.

BILL: Really?

JAMES: It's the smell I hate.

Pause.

BILL: Cheese? I've got a splendid cheese knife.

He picks up a cheese knife.

Look. Don't you think it's splendid?

JAMES: Is it sharp?

BILL: Try it. Hold the blade. It won't cut you. Not if you handle it properly. Not if you grasp it firmly up to the hilt.

JAMES does not touch the knife. BILL stands holding it.
Lights in house remain.
Fade up flat to full.

HARRY [*standing*]: Well, goodbye, I'm glad we've had our little chat.

STELLA: Yes.

HARRY: It's all quite clear now.

STELLA: I'm glad.

They move to door.

HARRY: Oh, Mr. Lloyd asked me if I would give you his best wishes . . . and sympathies.

He goes out. She stands still.

Goodbye.

Front door closes. STELLA lies on the sofa with kitten. She rests her head, is still.
Fade flat to half light.

BILL: What are you frightened of.

JAMES [*moving away*]: What's that?

BILL: What?

JAMES: I thought it was thunder.

BILL [*to him*]: Why are you frightened of holding this blade?

JAMES: I'm not frightened. I was just thinking of the thunder last week, when you and my wife were in Leeds.

BILL: Oh, not again, surely? I thought we'd left all that behind. Surely we have? You're not still worried about that, are you?

JAMES: Oh no. Just nostalgia, that's all.

BILL: Surely the wound heals when you know the truth, doesn't it? I mean, when the truth is verified? I would have thought it did.

JAMES: Of course.

BILL: What's there left to think about? It's a thing regretted, never to be repeated. No past, no future. Do you see what I mean? You're a chap who's been married for two years, aren't you, happily? There's a bond of iron between you and your wife. It can't be corroded by a trivial thing like this. I've apologized, she's apologized. Honestly, what more can you want?

Pause. JAMES *looks at him.* BILL *smiles.* HARRY *appears at front door, opens and closes it quietly, remains in the hall, unnoticed by the others.*

JAMES: Nothing.

BILL: Every woman is bound to have an outburst of . . . wild sensuality at one time or another. That's the way I look at it, anyway. It's part of their nature. Even though it may be the kind of sensuality of which you yourself have never been the fortunate recipient. What? [*He laughs.*] That is a husband's fate, I suppose. Mind you, I think it's the system that's at fault, not you. Perhaps she'll never need to do it again, who knows.

JAMES *stands, goes to fruit bowl, picks up fruit knife. He runs his finger along blade.*

JAMES: This is fairly sharp.

BILL: What do you mean?

JAMES: Come on.

BILL: I beg your pardon?

JAMES: Come on. You've got that one. I've got this one.

BILL: What about it?

JAMES: I get a bit tired of words sometimes, don't you? Let's have a game. For fun.

BILL: What sort of game?

JAMES: Let's have a mock duel.

BILL: I don't want a mock duel thank you.

JAMES: Of course you do. Come on. First one who's touched is a sissy.

BILL: This is all rather unsubtle, don't you think?

JAMES: Not in the least. Come on, into first position.

BILL: I thought we were friends.

JAMES: Of course we're friends. What on earth's the matter with you? I'm not going to kill you. It's just a game, that's all. We're playing a game. You're not windy, are you?

BILL: I think it's silly.

JAMES: I say, you've a bit of a spoilsport, aren't you?

BILL: I'm putting my knife down anyway.

JAMES: Well, I'll pick it up.

JAMES *does so and faces him with two knives.*

BILL: Now you've got two.

JAMES: I've got another one in my hip pocket.

Pause.

BILL: What do you do, swallow them?

JAMES: Do you?

Pause. They stare at each other.

[*Suddenly.*] Go on! Swallow it!

JAMES *throws knife at* BILL'S *face.* BILL *throws up hand to protect his face and catches knife, by blade. It cuts his hand.*

BILL: Ow!

JAMES: Well caught! What's the matter?

He examines BILL'S *hand.*

Let's have a look. Ah yes. Now you've got a scar on your hand. You didn't have one before, did you?

HARRY *comes into the room.*

HARRY [*entering*]: What have you done, nipped your hand?
Let's have a look. [*To* JAMES.] Only a little nip, isn't it?
It's his own fault for not ducking. I must have told him
dozens of times, you know, that if someone throws a knife
at you the silliest thing you can do is to catch it. You're
bound to hurt yourself, unless it's made of rubber. The
safest thing to do is duck. You're Mr. Horne?

JAMES: That's right.

HARRY: I'm so glad to meet you. My name's Harry Kane.
Bill been looking after you all right? I asked him to see
that you stayed until I got back, so glad you could spare
the time. What are we drinking? Whisky? Let's fill you up.
You and your wife run that little boutique down the road,
don't you? Funny we've never met, living so close, all in
the same trade, eh? Here you are. Got one, Bill? Where's
your glass? This one? Here . . . you are. Oh, stop rubbing
your hand, for goodness' sake. It's only a cheese knife.
Well, Mr. Horne, all the very best. Here's wishing us all
health, happiness and prosperity in the time to come, not
forgetting your wife, of course. Healthy minds in healthy
bodies. Cheers.

They drink.

By the way, I've just seen your wife, what a beautiful
kitten she has, you should see it, Bill, it's all white. We
had a very pleasant chat, your wife and I. Listen . . . old
chap . . . can I be quite blunt with you?

JAMES: Of course.

HARRY: Your wife . . . you see . . . made a little tiny confession
to me. I think I can use that word.

Pause.

BILL *is sucking his hand.*

What she confessed was . . . that she'd made the whole
thing up. She'd made the whole damn thing up. For some
odd reason of her own. They never met, you see, Bill and
your wife, they never even spoke. This is what Bill says,
and this is now what your wife admits. They had nothing
whatever to do with each other, they don't know each
other. Women are very strange. But I suppose you know
more about that than I do, she's your wife. If I were you
I'd go home and knock her over the head with a saucepan
and tell her not to make up such stories again.

Pause.

JAMES: She made the whole thing up, eh?

HARRY: I'm afraid she did.

JAMES: I see. Well, thanks very much for telling me.

HARRY: I thought it would be clearer for you, coming from
someone completely outside the whole matter.

JAMES: Yes. Thank you.

HARRY: Isn't that so, Bill?

BILL: Oh, quite so. I don't even know the woman. Wouldn't
know her if I saw her. Pure fantasy.

JAMES: How's your hand?

BILL: Not bad.

JAMES: Isn't it strange that you confirmed the whole of her
story?

BILL: It amused me to do so.

JAMES: Oh?

BILL: Yes. You amused me. You wanted me to confirm it.
It amused me to do so.

Pause.

HARRY: Bill's a slum boy, you see, he's got a slum sense of
humour. That's why I never take him along with me to
parties. Because he's got a slum mind. I have nothing
against slum minds per se, you understand, nothing at all.

There's a certain kind of slum mind which is perfectly all right in a slum, but when this kind of slum mind gets out of the slum it sometimes persists, you see, it rots everything. That's what Bill is. There's something faintly putrid about him, don't you find?

Pause.

Like a slug. There's nothing wrong with slugs, in their place, but he's a slum slug, there's nothing wrong with slum slugs in their place, but this one won't keep his place, he crawls all over the walls of nice houses, leaving slime, don't you boy? He confirms stupid sordid little stories just to amuse himself, while everyone else has to run round in circles to get to the root of the matter and smooth the whole thing out. All he can do is sit and suck his bloody hand and decompose like the filthy putrid slum slug he is. What about another whisky, Horne?

JAMES: No, I think I must be off now. Well, I'm glad to hear that nothing did happen. Great relief to me.

HARRY: It must be.

JAMES: My wife's not been very well lately, actually. Overwork.

HARRY: That's bad. Still you know what it's like in our business.

JAMES: Best thing to do is take her on a long holiday, I think.

HARRY: South of France.

JAMES: The Isles of Greece.

HARRY: Sun's essential, of course.

JAMES: I know. Bermuda.

HARRY: Perfect.

JAMES: Well, thanks very much, Mr. Kane, for clearing my mind. I don't think I'll mention it when I get home. Take her out for a drink or something. Forget all about it.

HARRY: Better hurry up. It's nearly closing time.

JAMES *moves to* BILL, *who is sitting.*

JAMES: I'm very sorry I cut your hand. You're lucky you caught it, of course. Otherwise it might have cut your mouth. Still, it's not too bad, is it?

Pause.

Look . . . I really think I ought to apologize for this silly story my wife made up. The fault is really all hers, and mine, for believing her. You're not to blame for taking it as you did. The whole thing must have been an impossible burden for you. What do you say we shake hands, as a testimony of my good will?

JAMES extends his hand. BILL rubs his cut right hand, does not extend it.

BILL: I never touched her . . . we sat . . . in the lounge, on a sofa . . . for two hours . . . talked . . . we talked about it . . . we didn't . . . move from the lounge . . . never went to her room . . . just talked . . . about what we would do . . . if we did get to her room . . . two hours . . . we never touched . . . we just talked about it . . .

Long silence.
JAMES leaves the house.
HARRY sits. BILL remains sitting, sucking his hand.
Silence.
Fade house to half light.
Fade up full on flat.
STELLA is lying with kitten. Flat door closes. JAMES comes in. He stands looking at her.

JAMES: You didn't do anything, did you?

Pause.

He wasn't in your room. You just talked about it, in the lounge.

Pause.

That's the truth, isn't it?

Pause.

You just sat and talked about what you would do, if you went to your room. That's what you did.

Pause.

Didn't you?

Pause.

That's the truth . . . isn't it?

STELLA *looks at him, neither confirming nor denying. Her face is friendly, sympathetic.*
Fade out to half light.
The four figures are still, in the half light.
Fade to blackout.

The Dwarfs

The Dwarfs was first performed on the B.B.C. Third Programme on 2 December 1960, with the following cast:

LEN   Richard Pasco
PETE   Jon Rollason
MARK   Alex Scott

Produced by Barbara Bray

The Dwarfs

The action of the play moves from MARK'S house to LEN'S house in a London suburb. LEN, PETE and MARK are all in their thirties.
The sound of a recorder being played. The sound is fragmentary.

LEN: Pete.

PETE: What?

LEN: Come here.

PETE: What?

LEN: What's the matter with this recorder? There's something wrong with this recorder.

PETE: Let's have some tea.

LEN: I can't do a thing with it.

Another attempt to play.

Where's the milk?

PETE: You were going to bring it.

LEN: That's right.

PETE: Well, where is it?

LEN: I forgot it. Why didn't you remind me?

PETE: Give me the cup.

LEN: What do we do now?

PETE: Give me the tea.

LEN: Without milk?

PETE: There isn't any milk.

LEN: What about sugar? [*Moving away.*] He must have a pint of milk somewhere.

Opening cupboards.

Here's a couple of gherkins. What about a gherkin? Fancy a gherkin. Wait a minute. Ah! Here we are. I knew he'd have a pint laid on.

Pressing the top.

Uuuh . . . uuuhh . . . it's stiff.

PETE: I wouldn't open that.

LEN: Uuuhh . . . why not? I can't drink tea without milk. Uuh! That's it. Give us your cup.

PETE: Leave it alone.

Pause.

LEN: It won't come out. [*Pause.*] The milk won't come out of the bottle.

PETE: It's been in there two weeks, why should it come out?

LEN: Two weeks? He's been away longer than two weeks. [*Slight pause.*] It's stuck in the bottle. [*Slight pause.*] You'd think a man like him would have a maid, wouldn't you, to look after the place while he's away, to look after his milk? Or a gentleman. A gentleman's gentleman. Are you quite sure he hasn't got a gentleman's gentleman tucked away somewhere, to look after the place for him?

PETE: Only you. You're the only gentleman's gentleman he's got.

Pause.

LEN: Well, if I'm his gentleman's gentleman I should have been looking after the place for him.

Pause.

PETE: What's this?

LEN: That? You've seen that before. It's a toasting fork.

PETE: It's got a monkey's head.

LEN: It's Portuguese. Everything in this house is Portuguese.

PETE: Why's that?

LEN: That's where he comes from.

PETE: So he does.

LEN: Or at least, his grandmother on his father's side. That's where the family comes from.

PETE: Yes.

LEN: What time's he coming?

PETE: Soon.

The recorder plays again.

What's the matter with that thing?

LEN: Nothing. There's nothing wrong with it. But it must be broken. It's a year since I played it. [*He sneezes.*] Aah! I've got the most shocking blasted cold I've ever had in all my life.

He blows his nose.

Still, it's not much of a nuisance, really.

PETE: Don't wear me out. [*Slight pause.*] Why don't you pull yourself together? You'll be ready for the loony bin next week if you go on like this.

Pause.

LEN: Ten to one he'll be hungry.

PETE: Who?

LEN: Mark. When he comes. He can eat like a bullock, that bloke. Still, he won't find much to come home to, will he? There's nothing in the kitchen, there's not even a bit of lettuce. It's like the workhouse here. [*Pause.*] He can eat like a bullock, that bloke. [*Pause.*] I've seen him finish off a loaf of bread before I'd got my jacket off. [*Pause.*] He'd never leave a breadcrumb on a plate in the old days. [*Pause.*] Of course, he may have changed. Things do change. But I'm the same. Do you know, I had five solid square meals one day last week? At eleven o'clock, two o'clock, six o'clock, ten o'clock and one o'clock. Not bad going. Work makes me hungry. I was working that day. [*Pause.*]

I'm always starving when I get up. Daylight has a funny effect on me. As for the night, that goes without saying. As far as I'm concerned the only thing you can do in the night is eat. It keeps me fit, especially if I'm at home. I have to run downstairs to put the kettle on, run upstairs to finish what I'm doing, run downstairs to cut a sandwich or arrange a salad, run upstairs to finish what I'm doing, run back downstairs to see to the sausages, if I'm having sausages, run back upstairs to finish what I'm doing, run back downstairs to lay the table, run back upstairs to finish what I'm doing, run back—

PETE: Yes!

LEN: Where did you get those shoes?

PETE: What?

LEN: Those shoes. How long have you had them?

PETE: What's the matter with them?

LEN: Have you been wearing them all night?

Pause.

PETE: When did you last sleep?

LEN: Sleep? Don't make me laugh. All I do is sleep.

PETE: What about work? How's work?

LEN: Euston? An oven. It's an oven. Still, bad air is better than no air. It's best on night shift. The trains come in, I give a bloke half a dollar, he does my job, I curl up in the corner and read the timetables. [*Pause.*] What are you doing with your hand?

PETE: What are you talking about?

LEN: What are you doing with your hand?

PETE [*coolly*]: What do you think I'm doing with it? Eh? What do you think?

LEN: I don't know.

PETE: I'll tell you, shall I? Nothing. I'm not doing anything with it. It's not moving. I'm doing *nothing* with it.

LEN: You're holding it palm upwards.

PETE: What about it?

LEN: It's not normal. Let's have a look at that hand. Let's have a look at it. [*Pause. He gasps through his teeth.*] You're a homicidal maniac.

PETE: Is that a fact?

LEN: Look. Look at that hand. Look, look at it. A straight line right across the middle. Right across the middle, see? Horizontal. That's all you've got. What else have you got? You're a nut.

PETE: Oh yes?

LEN: You couldn't find two men in a million with a hand like that. It sticks out a mile. A mile. That's what you are, that's exactly what you are, you're a homicidal maniac!

PETE: Ssshh! That's him.

A door slams. Voices of greeting, fading. Silence.

LEN: There is my table. That is a table. There is my chair. There is my table. That is a bowl of fruit. There is my chair. There are my curtains. There is no wind. It is past night and before morning. There is the coal-scuttle.

This is my room. This is a room. There is the wall-paper, on the walls. There are six walls. Eight walls. An octagon. This room is an octagon.

There are my shoes, on my feet.

There is no wind.

This is a journey and an ambush. This is the centre of the cold, a halt to the journey and no ambush. This is the deep grass I keep to. This is the thicket in the centre of the night and the morning. There is my hundred watt bulb like a dagger. It is neither night nor morning.

This room moves. This room is moving. It has moved. It has reached . . . a dead halt. The light on my skull places me in a manacle. This is my fixture. There is no web. All's clear, and abundant.

Perhaps a morning will arrive.

If a morning arrives, it will not destroy my fixture, nor
my luxury. If it is dark in the night or light, nothing ob-
trudes. I have my compartment. All is ordered, in its place,
no error has been made. I am wedged.
Here is my arrangement, and my kingdom. There are no
voices. They make no hole in my side.
[*Whispering.*] They make a hole, in my side.
[*Silence.*]
What's this, a suit? Where's your carnation?

MARK: What do you think of it?

LEN: It's not a schmutta.

MARK: It's got a zip at the hips.

LEN: A zip at the hips? What for?

MARK: Instead of a buckle. It's neat.

LEN: Neat? I should say it's neat.

MARK: No turn-ups.

LEN: I can see that. Why didn't you have turn-ups?

MARK: It's smarter without turn-ups.

LEN: Of course it's smarter without turn-ups.

MARK: I didn't want it double-breasted.

LEN: Double-breasted? Of course you couldn't have it double-
breasted.

MARK: What do you think of the cloth?

LEN: The cloth? [*He examines it, gasps and whistles through
his teeth. At a great pace.*] What a piece of cloth. What a
piece of cloth. What a piece of cloth. What a piece of cloth.
What a piece of *cloth*.

MARK: You like the cloth?

LEN: WHAT A PIECE OF CLOTH!

MARK: What do you think of the cut?

LEN: What do I think of the cut? The cut? The cut? What a
cut! What a cut! I've never seen such a cut! [*Pause. He
groans.*]

MARK: Do you know where I've just been?

LEN: Where?

MARK: Earl's Court.

LEN: Uuuuhh! What were you doing there? That's beside the point.

MARK: What's the matter with Earl's Court?

LEN: It's a mortuary without a corpse. [*Slight pause.*] There's a time and place for everything.

MARK: You're right there.

LEN: What do you mean by that?

MARK: There's a time and place for everything.

LEN: You're right there.

Pause.

MARK: I see that butter's going up.

LEN: I'm prepared to believe it, but it doesn't answer my question.

MARK: What was that?

LEN: What are you doing in my room? What do you want here?

MARK: I thought you might give me some bread and honey.

LEN: I don't want you to become too curious in this room. There's no place for curiosities here. Keep a sense of proportion. That's all I ask.

MARK: That's all.

LEN: I've got enough on my plate with this room as it is.

MARK: What's the matter with it?

LEN: The rooms we live in . . . open and shut. [*Pause.*] Can't you see? They change shape at their own will. I wouldn't grumble if only they would keep to some consistency. But they don't. And I can't tell the limits, the boundaries, which I've been led to believe are natural. I'm all for the natural behaviour of rooms, doors, staircases, the lot. But I can't rely on them. When, for example, I look through a train window, at night, and see the yellow lights, very clearly, I can see what they are, and I see that they're still. But they're only still because I'm moving. I know that they do move along with me, and when we go round a bend, they bump off. But I know that they are still, just the same. They are, after all, stuck on poles which are rooted to the earth. So they must be still, in their own right, insofar as the earth itself is still, which of course it isn't. The point is, in a nutshell, that I can only appreciate such facts when I'm moving. When I'm still, nothing around me follows a natural course of conduct. I'm not saying I'm any criterion, I wouldn't say that. After all, when I'm on that train I'm not really moving at all. That's obvious. I'm in the corner seat. I'm still. I am perhaps being moved, but I do not move. Neither do the yellow lights. The train moves, granted, but what's a train got to do with it?

MARK: Nothing.

LEN: You're frightened.

MARK: Am I?

LEN: You're frightened that any moment I'm liable to put a red hot burning coal in your mouth.

MARK: Am I?

LEN: But when the time comes, you see, what I shall do is place the red hot burning coal in my own mouth.

Silence.

I've got some beigels.

PETE: This is a very solid table, isn't it?

LEN: I said I've got some beigels.

PETE: No thanks. How long have you had this table?

LEN: It's a family heirloom.

PETE: Yes, I'd like a good table, and a good chair. Solid stuff. Made for the bearer. I'd put them in a boat. Sail it down the river. A houseboat. You could sit in the cabin and look out at the water.

LEN: Who'd be steering?

PETE: You could park it. Park it. There's not a soul in sight.

Pause.

LEN [*muttering*]: Impossible, impossible, impossible.

PETE [*briskly*]: I've been thinking about you.

LEN: Oh?

PETE: Do you know what your trouble is? You're not elastic. There's no elasticity in you. You want to be more elastic.

LEN: Elastic? Elastic. Yes, you're quite right. Elastic. What are you talking about?

PETE: Giving up the ghost isn't so much a failure as a tactical error. By elastic I mean being prepared for your own deviations. You don't know where you're going to come out next at the moment. You're like a rotten old shirt. Buck your ideas up. They'll lock you up before you're much older.

LEN: No. There is a different sky each time I look. The clouds run about in my eye. I can't do it.

PETE: The apprehension of experience must obviously be dependent upon discrimination if it's to be considered valuable. That's what you lack. You've got no idea how to preserve a distance between what you smell and what you think about it. You haven't got the faculty for making a simple distinction between one thing and another. Every time you walk out of this door you go straight over a cliff. What you've got to do is nourish the power of assessment. How can you hope to assess and verify anything if you walk about with your nose stuck between your feet all day long? You knock around with Mark too much. He can't do you any good. I know how to handle him. But I don't think he's your sort. Between you and me, I sometimes think he's a man of weeds. Though he does surprise me, now and again, for the good, I mean. But I sometimes think he's just playing a game. But what game? I like him, when you come down to it. You can forgive a lot. But you look at him and what do you see? An attitude. Has it substance or is it barren? Sometimes I think it's as barren as a bombed site. He'll be a spent force in no time if he doesn't watch his

step. [*Pause.*] I'll tell you a dream I had last night. I was
with a girl in a tube station, on the platform. People were
rushing about. There was some sort of panic. When I
looked round I saw everyone's faces were peeling, blotched,
blistered. People were screaming, booming down the
tunnels. There was a fire bell clanging. When I looked at
the girl I saw that her face was coming off in slabs too, like
plaster.

LEN *begins to grunt spasmodically, to whimper, hiss, and by
the end of the speech, to groan.*

Black scabs and stains. The skin was dropping off like
lumps of cat's meat. I could hear it sizzling on the electric
rails. I pulled her by the arm to get her out of there. She
wouldn't budge. Stood there, with half a face, staring at
me. I screamed at her to come away. Then I thought, Christ,
what's my face like? Is that why she's staring? Is that
rotting too?

LEN *groans.*

Silence.

LEN: The dwarfs are back on the job, keeping an eye on pro-
ceedings. They clock in very early, scenting the event. They
are like kites in a city disguise; they only work in cities.
Certainly they're skilled labourers, and their trade is not
without risk. They wait for a smoke signal and unpack their
kit. They're on the spot with no time wasted and circle the
danger area. There, they take up positions, which they are
able to change at a moment's notice. But they don't stop
work until the job in hand is ended, one way or another.
I have not been able to pay a subscription, but they've
consented to take me into their gang, on a short term basis.
I won't stay with them long. This assignment won't last
long. The game'll soon be up. All the same, it is essential
that I keep a close watch on the rate of exchange, on the

rise and fall of the market. Probably neither Pete nor Mark
knows to what extent the state of his exchange affects my
market. But it is so.

And so I shall keep the dwarfs company and watch with
them. They miss very little. With due warning from them
I shall be able to clear my stocks, should there be a land-
slide.

Silence.

MARK: Put that mirror back.

LEN: This is the best piece of furniture you've got in the house.
It's Spanish. No, Portuguese. You're Portuguese, aren't
you?

MARK: Put it back.

LEN: Look at your face in this mirror. Look. It's a farce.
Where are your features? You haven't got any features.
You couldn't call those features. What are you going to do
about it, eh? What's the answer?

MARK: Mind that mirror. It's not insured.

LEN: I saw Pete the other day. In the evening. You didn't
know that. I wonder about you. I often wonder about you.
But I must keep pedalling. I must. There's a time limit.
Who have you got hiding here? You're not alone here.
What about your Esperanto? Don't forget, anything over
two ounces goes up a penny.

MARK: Thanks for the tip.

LEN: Here's your mirror. Pete asked me to lend him a shilling.

MARK: Uh?

LEN: I refused.

MARK: What?

LEN: I refused downright to lend him a shilling.

MARK: What did he say to that?

LEN: Plenty. Since I left him I've been thinking thoughts
I've never thought before. I've been thinking thoughts I've
never thought before.

MARK: You spend too much time with Pete.

LEN: What?

MARK: Give it a rest. He doesn't do you any good. I'm the only one who knows how to get on with him. I can handle him. You can't. You take him too seriously. He doesn't worry me. I know how to handle him. He doesn't take any liberties with me.

LEN: Who said he takes liberties with me? Nobody takes liberties with me. I'm not the sort of man you can take liberties with.

MARK: You should drop it.

LEN: This is a funny toasting fork. Do you ever make any toast?

The fork drops on the hearth.

Don't touch it! You don't know what will happen if you touch it! You mustn't touch it! You mustn't bend! Wait. [*Pause.*] I'll bend. I'll . . . pick it up. I'm going to touch it. [*Pause. Softly.*] There. You see? Nothing happens when I touch it. Nothing. Nothing can happen. No one would bother. [*A broken sigh.*] You see, I can't see the broken glass. I can't see the mirror I have to look through. I see the other side. The other side. But I can't see the mirror side. [*Pause.*] I want to break it, all of it. But how can I break it? How can I break it when I can't see it?

Silence.

What are the dwarfs doing? They stumble in the gutters and produce their pocket watches. One with a face of chalk chucks the dregs of the daytime into a bin and seats himself on the lid. He is beginning to chew though he has not eaten. Now they collect at the back step. They scrub their veins at the running sink, now they are gorged in the sud. Spruced and preened, in time for the tuck. Time is kept to a T.

Under the kitchen window they all gobble the tinned milk.
They eat, too, in a chuckle of fingers. Backchat of bone,
crosstalk of bristled skin.
Pete talks. Mark talks. I talk. We sit. He stands.
The other stands. I stand.
He sits. The other talks. He talks. The other sits.
The other stands. I crouch.
He walks. The other sits.
He walks, talking. The other talks, sitting. He replies,
standing. I squat, say nothing.
He stands. The other sits. The other walks. The other
stands. They stand.
I speak, from a squatting position. No one replies.
I stand on my hands. They glance. They talk.
He walks to the kitchen. The other talks, sitting.
He comes back from the kitchen, places the teapot and cups.
The other questions. He replies.
I reply.
They glance, and smile, and talk, and walk, and talk.
I turn, bump, ricochet, dodge, retreat, pirouette.
The dwarfs squash their noses on the pane.
Pete and Mark drink their tea.
We watch.

Silence.

PETE: Thinking got me into this and thinking's got to get me
out. You know what I want? An efficient idea. You know
what I mean? An efficient idea. One that'll work. Something
I can pin my money on. An each way bet. Nothing's
guaranteed, I know that. But I'm willing to gamble. Look
at the sun and moon. What's the sun and moon but an
efficient idea?

LEN: The sun and moon? Efficient?

PETE: But you've got to be quite sure of what you mean by
efficient. Look at a nutcracker. You press the cracker and

the cracker cracks the nut. You might think that's an exact process. It's not. The nut cracks, but the hinge of the cracker gives out a friction which is completely incidental to the particular idea. It's unnecessary, an escape and wastage of energy to no purpose. So there's nothing efficient about a nutcracker.

Pause.

LEN: I squashed a tiny insect on a plate the other day. And I brushed the remains off my finger, with my thumb. Then I saw that the fragments were growing, like fluff. As they were falling, they were becoming larger, like fluff. I had put my hand into the body of a dead bird.

Silence.

They've gone on a picnic. They've time for picnics. They've left me to sweep the yard, to pacify the rats. No sooner do they leave, these dwarfs, than in come the rats. If the dwarfs take a holiday the rats take a holiday. At my expense, whichever way the wind blows. They've left me to attend to the abode, to make their landscape congenial. I can't do a good job. It's a hopeless task. The longer they stay the greater the mess. Nobody lifts a finger. Nobody gets rid of a damn thing. All their leavings pile up, pile mixing with pile. When they return from their picnics I tell them I've had a clearance, that I've been hard at it since their departure. They nod, they yawn, they gobble, they spew. They don't know the difference. In truth, I sit and stir the stumps, the skins, the bristle. I tell them I've slaved like a martyr, I've skivvied till I was black in the face, what about a tip, what about the promise of a bonus, what about a little something? They yawn, they show the blood stuck between their teeth, they play their scratching game, they tongue their chops, they bring in their nets, their webs, their traps, they make monsters of their innocent catch,

they gorge. Countless diversions. What about the job?
What about the job in hand? After all my devotion. What
about the rats I dealt with? What about the rats I saved
for you, that I plucked and hung out to dry, what about the
rat steak I tried all ways to please you? They won't touch
it, they don't see it. Where is it, they've hidden it, they're
hiding it till the time I can no longer stand upright and I
fall, they'll bring it out then, grimed then, green, varnished,
rigid, and eat it as a victory dish.

Silence.

MARK: Why don't you put it on the table? What's up your
nose now?

LEN: What do you want me to say?

MARK: Open it up, Len. I can't see you for the cobwebs.

LEN: I'm in the centre of a holy plague.

MARK: Shall I send out a cart to bury the dead?

LEN: Sometimes you're a snake to me.

MARK: Take it easy.

LEN: You're a snake in my house.

MARK: Really?

LEN: You're trying to buy and sell me. You think I'm a
ventriloquist's dummy. You've got me pinned to the wall
before I open my mouth. You've got a tab on me, you're
buying me out of house and home, you're a calculating
bastard. [*Pause.*] Answer me. Say something. [*Pause.*] Do
you understand? [*Pause.*] You don't agree? [*Pause.*] You
disagree? [*Pause.*] You think I'm mistaken? [*Pause.*] But
am I? [*Pause.*] You're too big for me. You and Pete, you're
too big. Sometimes I'm all right. And then the room
becomes full of ice. I don't understand Pete, but I can feel
him at a distance, sometimes. You I can seldom feel at a
distance and I don't understand you, either. You're not as
simple as you look. Both of you bastards, you've made a
hole in my side, I can't plug it! [*Pause.*] I've lost a kingdom.

I respond, you see, to the intimate and minute. If only I could close my eyes and live alone with suggestions of life. I can't manage when the world begins to bang. I suppose you're taking good care of things. Did you know that you and Pete are a music hall act? What happens? What do you do when you're alone? Do you do a jig? I suppose you're taking good care of things. For me, you see, I don't grow old. I change. I don't die. I change again. I am not happy. I change. Nor unhappy. But when a big storm takes place I do not change. I become someone else, which means I change out of all recognition, I am transformed from the world in which I suffer the changes I suffer, I retreat utterly from the standpoint where I am subject to change, then with my iron mask on I wait for the storm to pass. But at the same time it is, I admit, impossible in these moments to sit quite still without wanting to go back. It's also impossible not to feel the itch to go forward. I must learn restraint. I suppose you're taking good care of things. I've got my treasure too. It's in my corner. Everything's in my corner. Everything is from the corner's point of view. I don't hold the whip. I'm a labouring man. I do the corner's will. I slave my guts out. I thought, at one time, that I'd escaped it, but it never dies, it's never dead. I feed it. It's well fed. Things that at one time seem to me of value I have no resource but to give it to eat and what was of value turns into pus. I can hide nothing. I can't lay anything aside. Nothing can be put aside, nothing can be hidden, nothing can be saved, it waits, it eats, it's voracious, you're in it, Pete's in it, you're all in my corner. There must be somewhere else!

Silence.

Easy come easy go. They are not bothered, these dwarfs, never at a loose end. The tiniest substances, the prettiest trifles, nourish and sustain them. Now there is a new game, to do with beetles and twigs. There is a rockery of red hot cinder. The hairs are curled and oily on their necks. Always squatting and bending, dipping their wicks in the custard. Home methods are the best. I stand wafted by odours, in the shadows. From time to time a lick of flame screws up their nostrils. They yowl, they scutter to the sandpit, pinch, dribble, chew, whimper, gouge, then soothe each other's orifices with a local ointment, and then, all gone, all forgotten, they lark about, each with his buddy. High life. One time I wangled a spoonful of porridge. It was like nothing I've ever tasted. Out on its own. No one dwarf is chef. It's a brotherhood. A true community. They even have hymn singing. Evenings round the bonfire. Now we have the nose spray, the scented syringe. Back to the beetle game, back to the cooking. So I note their progress. So I commend their industry. So I applaud their motive. So I trust their efficiency. So I find them capable.

Silence.

Pete walks by the river. Under the woodyard wall stops. Stops. Hiss of the yellow grass. The wood battlements jaw over the wall. Dust in the fairground ticks. The night ticks. He hears the tick of the roundabout, up river with the sweat. What is he doing? He squats, by the shoreside. Ball of a boulder. Leave it. Leave it. He's at it, scrabbles under it, wrenching, lifts, pulls, u-u-u-u-u-p. Beetles in the yawn. A crash of water. The river jolts from his boot.
Pete walks by the river. Under the woodyard wall stops. Stops. The wood hangs. Deathmask on the water.
Pete walks by the — gull. Slicing gull. Gull. Down. He stops. Stone. Watches. Rat corpse in the yellow grass. Gull pads. Gull probes. Gull stamps his feet. Gull whinnies up. Gull screams, tears, Pete tears, digs, Pete cuts, breaks, Pete stretches the corpse, flaps his wings, Pete's beak grows, probes, digs, pulls, the river jolts, no moon, what can I see,

the dwarfs collect, they slide down the bridge, they scutter by the shoreside, the dwarfs collect, capable, industrious, they wear raincoats, it is going to rain, Pete digs, he screws in to the head, the dwarfs watch, Pete tugs, he tugs, he's tugging, he kills, he's killing, the rat's head, with a snap the cloth of the rat's head tears.

Pete walks by the . . . [*Deep groan.*]

Silence.

PETE: You look the worse for wear. What's the matter with you?

LEN: I've been ill.

PETE: Ill? What was the matter?

LEN: Cheese. Stale cheese. It got me in the end. I've been eating a lot of cheese.

PETE: Yes, well, it's easy to eat too much cheese.

LEN: It all came out, in about twenty-eight goes. I couldn't stop shivering and I couldn't stop squatting. It got me all right. I'm all right now. I only go three times a day now. I can more or less regulate it. Once in the morning. A quick dash before lunch. Another quick dash after tea, and then I'm free to do what I want. I don't think you can understand. That cheese didn't die. It only began to live when you swallowed it, you see, after it had gone down. I bumped into a German one night, he came home with me and helped to finish it off. He took it to bed with him, he sat up in bed with it, in the guest's room. I went in and had a gander. He had it taped. He was brutal with it. He would bite into it and then concentrate. I had to hand it to him. The sweat came out on his nose but he stayed on his feet. After he'd got out of bed, that was. Stood bolt upright. Swallowed it, clicked his fingers, ordered another piece of blackcurrant pie. It's my pie-making season. His piss stank worse than Old Testament Rabbis. You look in the pink.

PETE: You want to watch your step. You know that? You're going from bad to worse. Why don't you pull yourself together? Eh? Get a steady job. Cultivate a bit of go and guts for a change. Make yourself useful, mate, for Christ's sake. As you are, you're just a dead weight round everybody's neck.

Silence.

LEN: Mark sits by the fireside. Crosses his legs. His fingers wear a ring. The finger poised. Mark regards his finger. He regards his legs. He regards the fireside. Outside the door is the black blossom. He combs his hair with an ebony comb, He sits, he lies, he lowers his eyelashes, raises them, sees no change in the posture of the room, lights a cigarette, watches his hand clasp the lighter, watches the flame, sees his mouth go forward, sees the consumation, is satisfied. Pleased, sees the smoke in the lamp, pleased with the lamp and the smoke and his bulk, pleased with his legs and his ring and his hand and his body in the lamp. Sees himself speaking, the words arranged on his lips, sees himself with pleasure silent.

Under the twigs they slide, by the lilac bush, break the stems, sit, scutter to the edge of the lawn and there wait, capable, industrious, put up their sunshades, watch.

Mark lies, heavy, content, watches his smoke in the window, times his puff out, his hand fall, [*with growing disgust*] smiles at absent guests, sucks in all comers, arranges his web, lies there a spider.

Silence.

What did you say?

MARK: I never said anything.

LEN: What do you do when you're tired, go to bed?

MARK: That's right.

LEN: You sleep like a log.

MARK: Yes.

LEN: What do you do when you wake up?

MARK: Wake up.

LEN: I want to ask you a question.

MARK: No doubt.

LEN: Are you prepared to answer questions?

MARK: No.

LEN: What do you do in the day when you're not walking about?

MARK: I rest.

LEN: Where do you find a resting place?

MARK: Here and there.

LEN: By consent?

MARK: Invariably.

LEN: But you're not particular?

MARK: Yes, I'm particular.

LEN: You choose your resting place?

MARK: Sometimes.

LEN: That might be anywhere?

MARK: Yes.

LEN: Have you a home?

MARK: No.

LEN: What did you say?

MARK: No.

LEN: So where are you?

MARK: Between homes.

LEN: Do you believe in God?

MARK: What?

LEN: Do you believe in God?

MARK: Who?

LEN: God.

MARK: God?

LEN: Do you believe in God?

MARK: Do I believe in God?

LEN: Yes.

MARK: Would you say that again?

LEN: Have a biscuit.

MARK: Thanks.

LEN: They're your biscuits.

MARK: There's two left. Have one yourself.

LEN: You don't understand. You'll never understand.

MARK: Really?

LEN: Do you know what the point is? Do you know what it is?

MARK: No.

LEN: The point is, who are you? Not why or how, not even what. I can see what, perhaps, clearly enough. But who are you? It's no use saying you know who you are just because you tell me you can fit your particular key into a particular slot which will only receive your particular key because that's not foolproof and certainly not conclusive. Just because you're inclined to make these statements of faith has nothing to do with me. It's not my business. Occasionally I believe I perceive a little of what you are but that's pure accident. Pure accident on both our parts, the perceived and the perceiver. It's nothing like an accident, it's deliberate, it's a joint pretence. We depend on these accidents, on these contrived accidents, to continue. It's not important then that it's conspiracy or hallucination. What you are, or appear to be to me, or appear to be to you, changes so quickly, so horrifyingly, I certainly can't keep up with it and I'm damn sure you can't either. But who you are I can't even begin to recognize, and sometimes I recognize it so wholly, so forcibly, I can't look, and how can I be certain of what I see? You have no number. Where am I to look, where am I to look, what is there to locate, so as to have some surety, to have some rest from this whole bloody racket? You're the sum of so many reflections. How many reflections? Whose reflections? Is that what you consist of? What scum does the tide leave? What happens to the scum? When does it happen? I've seen what happens. But I can't speak when I see it. I can only point a finger. I can't even do that. The scum is broken and sucked back. I don't see where it goes, I don't see when, what do I see, what have I seen? What have I seen, the scum or the essence? What about it? Does all this give you the right to stand there and tell me you know who you are? It's a bloody impertinence. There's a great desert and there's a wind stopping. Pete's been eating to much cheese, he's ill from it, it's eating his flesh away, but that doesn't matter, you're still both in the same boat, you're eating all my biscuits, but that doesn't matter, you're still both in the same boat, you're still standing behind the curtains together. He thinks you're a fool, Pete thinks you're a fool, but that doesn't matter, you're still both of you standing behind my curtains, moving my curtains in my room. He may be your Black Knight, you may be his Black Knight, but I'm cursed with the two of you, with two Black Knights, that's friendship, that's this that I know. That's what I know.

MARK: Pete thinks I'm a fool? [*Pause.*] Pete . . . Pete thinks that I'm a *fool*?

Silence.

PETE: Hullo, Mark.
MARK: Hullo.
PETE: What are you doing?
MARK: Nothing.
PETE: Going to invite me in.
MARK: Sure.

Pause.

PETE: Well, what are you doing with yourself?
MARK: When's that?
PETE: Now.
MARK: Nothing.

Pause.

PETE: Len's in hospital.

MARK: Len? What's the matter with him?

PETE: Kidney trouble. Not serious. [*Pause.*] Well, what have you been doing with yourself?

MARK: When?

PETE: Since I saw you.

MARK: This and that.

PETE: This and what?

MARK: That.

Pause.

PETE: Do you want to go and see Len?

MARK: When? Now?

PETE: Yes. It's visiting time. [*Pause.*] Are you busy?

MARK: No.

Pause.

PETE: What's up?

MARK: What?

PETE: What's up?

MARK: What do you mean?

PETE: You're wearing a gasmask.

MARK: Not me.

Pause.

PETE: Ready?

MARK: Yes.

Steps on the road.

PETE: Fine day. [*Pause.*] Bit chilly.

Hospital sounds.

LEN: You got here.

PETE: Yes.

LEN: They can't do enough for me here.

PETE: Why's that?

LEN: Because I'm no trouble. They treat me like a king. These nurses, they treat me exactly like a king. [*Pause.*] Mark looks as though he's caught a crab.

MARK: Do I?

PETE: Airy, this ward.

LEN: Best quality blankets, home cooking, everything you could wish for. Look at the ceiling. It's not too high and it's not too low.

Pause.

PETE: By the way, Mark, what happened to your pipe?

MARK: Nothing happened to it.

Pause.

LEN: You smoking a pipe? [*Pause.*] What's it like out today?

PETE: Bit chilly.

LEN: Bound to be.

PETE: The sun's come out.

LEN: The sun's come out? [*Pause.*] Well, Mark, bring off the treble chance this week?

MARK: Not me.

Pause.

LEN: Who's driving the tank?

PETE: What?

LEN: Who's driving the tank?

PETE: Don't ask me. We've been walking up the road back to back.

LEN: You've what? [*Pause.*] You've been walking up the road back to back? [*Pause.*] What are you doing sitting on my bed? You're not supposed to sit on the bed, you're supposed to sit on the chairs!

Steps on the road.

PETE: Horizontal personalities, those places. You're the only vertical. Makes you feel dizzy. [*Pause.*] You ever been inside one of those places?

MARK: I can't remember.

PETE: Right.

[*Pause.*]

MARK: All right. Why do you knock on my door?

PETE: What?

MARK: Come on. Why do you knock on my door?

PETE: What are you talking about?

MARK: Why?

PETE: I call to see you.

MARK: What do you want with me? Why come and see me?

PETE: Why?

MARK: You're playing a double game. You've been playing a double game. You've been using me. You don't give a tinker's shit for any of us.

PETE: Mind how you go.

MARK: You've been wasting my time, you've been leading me up the garden. For years.

PETE: Don't push me, boy.

MARK: You think I'm a fool.

PETE: Is that what I think?

MARK: That's what you think. You think I'm a fool.

PETE: You are a fool.

MARK: You've always thought that.

PETE: From the beginning.

MARK: You've been leading me up the garden.

PETE: And you.

MARK: You know what you are? You're an infection.

PETE: Don't believe it. All I've got to do to destroy you is to leave you as you wish to be.

Silence.

LEN: They've stopped eating. It'll be a quick get out when the whistle blows. All their belongings are stacked in piles. They've doused the fire. But I've heard nothing. What is the cause for alarm? Why is everything packed? Why are they ready for the off?

But they say nothing. Either they've gone dumb or I've gone deaf. Or they've gone deaf and I've gone dumb. Or we're neither dumb nor deaf. In that case it's a conspiracy pure and simple. They've cut me off without a penny.

And now they've settled down to a wide-eyed kip, cross-legged by the fire. It's insupportable. I'm left in the lurch. Not even a stale frankfurter, a slice of bacon rind, a leaf of cabbage, not even a mouldy piece of salami, like they used to sling me in the days when we told old tales by suntime. They sit, chock-full. But I smell a rat. They seem to be anticipating a rarer dish, a choicer spread.

And this change. All about me the change. The yard as I know it is littered with scraps of cat's meat, pig bollocks, tin cans, bird brains, spare parts of all the little animals, a squelching squealing carpet, all the dwarfs' leavings spittled in the muck, worms stuck in the poisoned shit heaps, the alleys a whirlpool of piss, slime, blood, and fruit juice.

Now all is bare. All is clean. All is scrubbed. There is a lawn. There is a shrub. There is a flower.

A List of Evergreen Books

E368 **FICCIONES** — Borges — $2.45
E370 **EDUCATION FOR FREEDOM** — Hutchins — $1.45
E373 **HITLER'S SECRET BOOK** — $2.45
E374 **THE SCREENS** — Genet — $1.95
E375 **HELEN IN EGYPT** — H.D. — $2.45
E377 **MODERN GERMAN POETRY** — Hamburger, Middleton, eds. — $2.95
E378 **FILM: BOOK 2** — Hughes, ed. — $2.45
E379 **POEMS IN ENGLISH** — Beckett — $1.45
E380 **THE PHYSICISTS** — Dürrenmatt — $1.75
E381 **TOM JONES** — Osborne — $1.95
E382 **STAND UP, FRIEND, WITH ME** — Field — $1.45
E383 **TOWARD JAZZ** — Hodeir — $1.95
E384 **SYSTEMATIC SOCIOLOGY** — Mannheim — $1.75
E385 **TROPIC OF CAPRICORN** — Miller — $2.45
E386 **THE DEAD LECTURER** — LeRoi Jones — $1.45
E387 **NOTES & COUNTER NOTES** — Ionesco — $2.45
E388 **HOW IT IS** — Beckett — $1.95
E389 **WHAT IS EXISTENTIALISM?** — Barrett — $1.95
E390 **THE WRETCHED OF THE EARTH** — Fanon — $1.95
E391 **BERTHA AND OTHER PLAYS** — Koch — $1.95
E392 **THE ERASERS** — Robbe-Grillet — $1.95
E393 **ENTERTAINING MR. SLOANE** — Joe Orton — $1.45
E394 **SQUARE IN THE EYE** — Gelber — $1.95
E397 **THE STRUCTURE AND DYNAMICS OF ORGANIZATIONS AND GROUPS** — Berne — $2.45
E398 **SAN FRANCISCO AT YOUR FEET** — Doss — $1.95
E399 **INADMISSIBLE EVIDENCE** — Osborne — $1.75

If your bookseller doesn't have these books, you may order them by writing
to Order Dept., Grove Press, Inc., 80 University Place, New York, New
York 10003. Please enclose cash and add 25¢ for postage and handling.